# Horse Rider's Mechanic

# Workbook 1:

# Your Position

Jane Myers

Equiculture Publishing

Edition 1

**Equiculture Publishing**

ISBN 978-0994156105

# Disclaimer

The author and publisher shall have neither liability nor responsibility to any person or entity with respect to any loss or damage or injury caused or alleged to be caused directly or indirectly by the information contained in this book. While the book is as accurate as the author can make it, there may be errors, omissions, and inaccuracies.

# Also by Equiculture Publishing

Horse Rider's Mechanic Workbook 2: Your Balance

A horse is a horse of course: a guide to equine behaviour

Horse pasture management

Understanding horses and pasture

Horse property planning

Buying a horse property

Manure, water and vegetation on a horse property

Riding arenas and training yards

Stables, yards and shelters

Horse property fences and gates

Horse properties - a management guide

**These books are available as ebooks and printed from the shops on our websites, www.horseridersmechanic.com and www.equiculture.com.au**

**New books are becoming available all the time, make sure you sign up for our mailing list while you are on our websites so that you find out when they are published.**

# Contents

# By reading this book you will...

## Improve performance

You and your horse will work better together. You will improve your position, balance and application of the aids. This will give your horse a better understanding of what he or she is meant to do and you will both be able to perform better (whatever you do together). A never ending upwards spiral!

## Increase your safety and security

Riding is classed as one of the more dangerous sports and pastimes. In particular the position and balance of a rider are inextricably linked. In turn they determine how safe and secure a rider is. With the help of these books you will now be able to give yourself a whole body 'tune up' and your safety and security will improve greatly because of it. Think of it as putting your body through a thorough check-up followed by making adjustments based on what you have found.

## Enjoy your riding more

Becoming a better rider will lead to more enjoyment as you experience 'light bulb moments' over and over again. Learning is fun as you just keep getting better. Your horse will move more freely as he or she learns that you are becoming easier to carry. A comfortable horse that is not stressed is more fun (and safer) to ride.

## Save money

Improving your riding takes time, patience and money. It is a very apt saying that if you look after the basics (the foundations) then what follows will look after itself. The **Horse Rider's Mechanic** series of workbooks focuses on the foundations. Without good solid foundations, nothing substantial can be built. Riding is an expensive sport or pastime. We are not saying you should cut corners however these books will help you to progress in such a way that any instruction that you do have will be more cost effective because you will have better foundations.

## Reduce or eliminate stress for your horse

A rider has the potential to inflict a huge amount of stress on a horse – in so many ways. At Equiculture we teach people how to minimise or eliminate that stress. Our main website **www.equiculture.com.au** deals with the horse management side of stress reduction. This series of books (and the Horse Rider's Mechanic website that supports them, **www.horseridersmechnic.com**) are about how you can reduce or eliminate that stress when riding.

So much is discussed and written about how important it is for a horse to be 'straight', 'supple', 'balanced and 'relaxed'. This series of books teaches you how to make sure that you uphold your part of the bargain - by working to be the best rider you can be. Whatever your riding interests, whether you ride just for fun or to compete (or both), it is important that you ride to the best of your ability.

## A rider's responsibilities

### As a horse owner/rider you should ensure that your horse is free from stress and pain.

A domestic horse should be kept in such a way that does not cause stress. Any horse that is being used for riding should be fit, strong and well enough for the purpose. The horse should be trained enough so that he or she is capable of performing the required task. The horse should be fed correctly, have correct hoof care, teeth care, skin care etc. All gear that is used on the horse (for riding or handling) should fit correctly and should not inflict pain.

### All of these subjects and more are covered by articles and books on the Horse Rider's Mechanic website www.horseridersmechanic.com and on our other website www.equiculture.com.au

A rider should aim to improve their position and balance and method of signalling ('aids') so that the horse finds it as easy as possible to carry the rider and understands what he or she is being asked to do. A rider should aim to keep learning so that they can continue to improve their horse management and rider skills.

## Support

Remember, there are many articles on *www.horseridersmechanic.com* that support the information in this book. It is up to you whether you read them first or read them as they are referred to in the text. They include subjects such as *Your safety, Your confidence, Your horse, Your horse's gear, Your body, Your riding area* and *Your assistant*. There are many others listed on the same page that you should find interesting.

**In addition: if there is anything you do not understand or need help with after reading this book (or the others in this series) post a question on the Horse Rider's Mechanic Facebook page:**

**www.facebook.com/horseridersmechanic**

**This Facebook page is especially for the readers of these books. Help is at hand!**

**You may never have come across this kind of information before (at least not in the way it is presented in the Horse Rider's Mechanic series of books) so I hope you enjoy this new 'journey' that you are about to take as have indeed so many of my clients in the past!**

## A further disclaimer

Just to remind you, I am *not* a human body worker (physiotherapist etc.) but a horse riding instructor that specialises in dealing with horse rider position and balance issues. Therefore I am very interested in human biomechanics and I talk/write extensively on this subject, but this does not make me a doctor or any other type of human health expert. Make sure you have any real problems with your body checked out by a professional (i.e. a physiotherapist etc).

# How to get the most from this book

Now we will look at how we can 'tune' the various parts of your body in detail. The information in the following sections is thorough and detailed but if you simply read the rest of this book and then attempt to make changes from what you remember, you may miss some very important points. I suggest you do the following to maximise your chances of succeeding in your quest to improve your riding:

- Start by reading through the rest of this book *at least* once. As you go through it identify your own particular problems.
- Obtain some small cards (such as blank postcards) and copy the information that describes what each part of your body *should* actually do (each one is only a few dot points long and writing them down will help to consolidate the points in your mind).
- Number the cards starting with number one for your feet.
- Make sure you write them all down, even if you think you do not have a problem with that particular body part.
- On your personalised cards also write the solution (from this book) to your own particular problem.
- Take the cards with you when you next ride and starting with card number one, work through them. This may take many sessions or you may get through them quite quickly, take as long as you need (if you are working through this book with an assistant they can read the cards out to you while you ride).

4

- Aim to concentrate on *one area at a time*, no more. So start at your feet and so on, only moving on to the next part of your body when you are confident about understanding and applying what is required for the current body part.
- As already mentioned, for some people the whole process may take little time, for others much longer. You will be surprised at what you learn about your riding by doing this. For most riders this is the first time they will have given so much attention to each part of their body in turn and when they do the results can be quite an eye opener but remember time is not the issue, learning the correct feel and improving your position is.
- As you ride around in a circle (once you have warmed up your horse and yourself), begin by turning as much of your attention, as it is safe to do so, to each part of your body in the order that they appear on the cards. Even if you do not think you have a problem with for instance, your ankles, do not skip the mental check of this area of your body. You may be amazed at what you learn as you do this and if you skip this area you may miss a vital clue or solution.
- A common instruction I have given while working through the various areas is to *experiment* with different amounts of muscle tension in each part of your body. By increasing tension and then decreasing it you should find that you begin to notice what is correct for you.
- Good riding involves achieving the right amount of muscle tension in each area of your body, not too little and not too much. Another way of putting it is that you need to be not too loose or too stiff to ride well. You can only learn this through 'trial and error'. Remember everyone is an individual. Only you can experiment and learn what your body needs by making an area of your body more 'still' or making an area more 'loose' and noticing if this improves your riding.

- Once you have worked your way through the cards start at the beginning and work through them again, *at least one more time*. This is important because as you make adjustments to parts of your body, other areas may try to compensate and you may end up 'undoing' an area that you previously corrected. As you learn to be more intuitive about your body as a rider you will be able to make minor adjustments quite easily in time, but at first you will need to apply quite a bit of concentration to do this.
- Don't attempt to 'school' your horse at the same time you are doing these positional checks as this will prevent you from concentrating properly on the various feelings that you need for feedback (see the Horse Rider's Mechanic website article **Your horse**). This feedback will give you the information that you need to make any necessary changes. For these sessions your horse is simply helping you to improve as a rider which in turn will benefit your horse enormously in the future.

**Remember: it is a good idea to read through the articles on www.horseridersmechanic.com. These articles will prepare you for the instructions in this book.**

**Have a look at the Horse Rider's Mechanic Facebook page: www.facebook.com/horseridersmechanic**

**You can post any questions that you have as you work through this book and the others in this series.**

**Here we go!**

# 1: Your feet

Your feet are a *very* important part of your riding anatomy. You might think that you ride on your 'seat', therefore you simply 'sit' on a horse, whereas this is not the case. Riding *well* involves developing the correct *weighting* between your seat *and* your feet. That is not to say that you should be *pressing downwards* through your seat or your feet, not at all, it is simply about *properly distributing* the downwards force of gravity that is acting on your body.

## 1.1: Your feet should...

- Rest in the stirrups, *without pressing down on them*. Utilised properly, the weight of your legs is enough to do this.
- Maintain the correct amount of downward pressure to keep the stirrup treads *directly* under the balls of your feet.
- Feel the same. There should not be more pressure on one foot than the other.
- Be only slightly lower in the heels than the toes (picture a). Your heels should not be forced down.

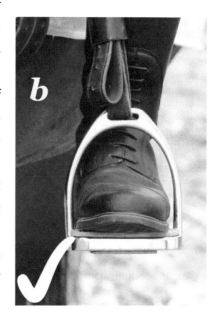

to the ground from side to side (picture b, previous
tirrup treads *and* the balls of your feet should both be
e ground.

s pointing straight or almost straight forward. Again
ion should not be forced.

- Give you the feeling of security.

*As you can see in the picture below, your feet have numerous parts to them. There are many bones and many soft tissues (tendons and ligaments).*

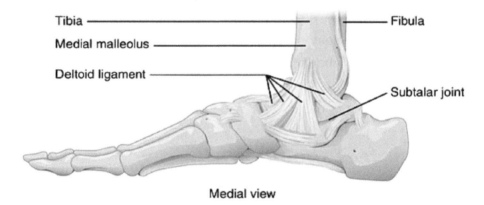

Tibia — Fibula
Medial malleolus —
Deltoid ligament —
— Subtalar joint

**Medial view**

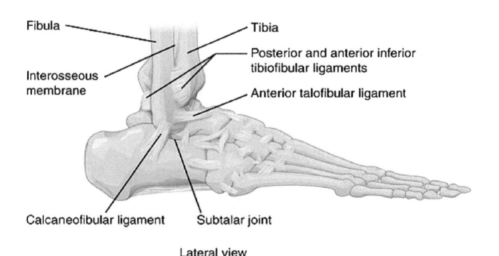

Fibula — Tibia
— Posterior and anterior inferior tibiofibular ligaments
Interosseous membrane —
— Anterior talofibular ligament

Calcaneofibular ligament    Subtalar joint

**Lateral view**

# 1.2: However your feet may...

- Be too low in the heels and therefore have reduced shock absorbency potential (this problem is due to 'problem ankles' and will be covered in that section).

*If your heels are jammed down you will lose the shock absorbing function of your ankles (because they are already at full stretch). Riding in this way also pushes your feet too far forward.*

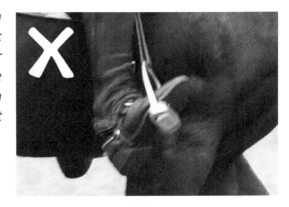

- Be unlevel (tilt from side to side).
- Go numb (especially in the 'outside' toes).
- Point outwards too much.
- Be painful (usually through the instep).
- Have uneven weighting (more weight in one foot).
- Keep losing the stirrups. This may involve either one or both stirrups and may be either fully or partially (i.e. the stirrup/s move around and/or twist on your feet).

*Your stirrups should stay in the correct position on your feet without you having to think about them. They should not move around or come off your feet while you are riding.*

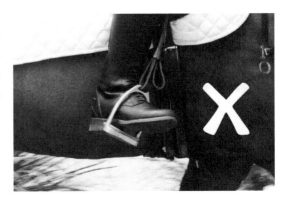

# 1.3: What you can do if...

## 1.3.1: ...feet are unlevel (from side to side)

If your feet tilt then this may mean that you are twisting all of the joints in your legs to some degree.

If you have an assistant they should be able to see that your stirrup treads *and* the balls of your feet are parallel to the ground. They could take a photo of your feet from the front so that you can see what they see. Alternatively arena mirrors will help you to check.

*When a rider tilts their foot a gap can be seen between the stirrup tread and their boot on the inside of the foot. Instead, all of the ball of their foot should make contact with the stirrup tread.*

If you are on a round barrelled horse and you have very short legs (this tends to occur in children rather than adults) it may not be achievable to have the stirrup treads parallel to the ground but the idea is that you should not be *forcing* your feet to tilt one way or the other. Be *very* wary about using wedged stirrup treads.

*It is not usually a good idea to force your feet to tilt one way or the other. This style of wedges rarely seem to be beneficial and many riders report that they have caused pain.*

Riders usually benefit from replacing wedges with flat stirrup treads and being shown how to weight their feet correctly instead (a person with a pre prescribed medical condition could be an exception).

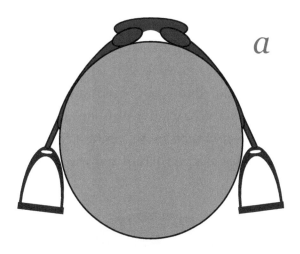

On the other hand, in the case of the earlier scenario (round barrelled horse, short legs, causing the base of the stirrup irons to tilt incorrectly) (picture a), a wedge or small bandage wrapped around the stirrup treads in order to *level* the stirrup treads (rather than tip them too far the other way) can help (picture b). Experiment with what feels comfortable.

## Solutions

- Once you have ensured that your stirrups treads are parallel to the ground, think about what you can feel under the ball of each foot.
- When you have discovered what you feel, if it is not correct, concentrate on weighting your feet so that you can feel the *entire* stirrup bar under the ball of each foot, not just the outside edge of it.

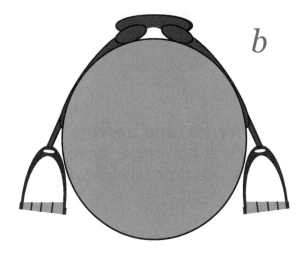

- If you have been riding with your feet tilted for some time it may feel very strange to level the pressure across your feet. In fact you might have to deliberately weight the *inside* of your feet at first (picture below).

- When you think that you have it, work on something else for a while. Return to concentrating on your feet and notice if you have reverted back to weighting just the outside of your feet.

- Keep practising this until it feels 'normal' to weight the *whole* of the ball of each foot and you no longer have to correct them.

*Remember: when you make any changes to your position the new feeling will probably feel quite strange at first. This is because part of your brain is telling your body to go back to doing 'the wrong thing' (the old 'normal') while another part of your brain is trying to override that instruction to get your body to do 'the right thing' (the new 'normal'). Once your brain 'learns' and accepts this new feeling (and 'files' it) you will no longer have to concentrate to maintain the new position, weighting etc. and it will start to feel fine.*

## 1.3.2: ...feet are numb

Tilting the feet as described in the previous section often leads to 'dead' toes on the 'outside' toes of the feet. This tilting can come about because the rider is trying to 'wrap' their legs around their horse. This is often because they were told to do this when being taught to ride (picture a).

A rider may also have been instructed to point their toes *in* while riding. Doing this can also put an unnatural twist on all of joints in their legs (picture b). It is usually physically impossible for a rider to actually wrap their

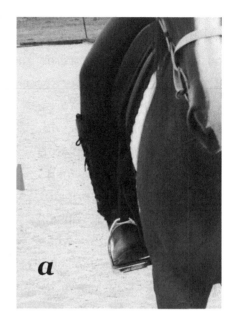

*a*

legs around a horse but while trying to do this they end up *rolling* their ankles to the outside. This problem is exacerbated further if a rider has loose wobbly ankles. The solution to this problem is dealt with in *2.3.1: ...ankles are wobbly*.

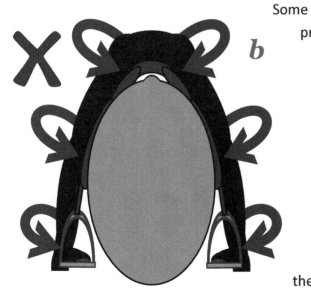

*b*

Some riders have equal pressure across the balls of their feet but they press *down* into the stirrups in an attempt to not lose them. It is impossible to have the correct relationship with the stirrups by *pressing down* on them. The weight of a rider's legs resting in the stirrups creates enough downward pressure to keep them on the feet (once the joints of the legs behave properly) without the rider having to press. As well as causing numbness, riding like this pushes the weight *upwards* and therefore *raises* the centre of gravity (CoG). See the Horse Rider's Mechanic website article ***Your centre of gravity***.

This problem tends to be more common in riders with stiff ankles because the stiffness prevents the ankles from dipping and springing back as they should. You will read more about this when you get to the relevant section.

*This rider is pushing down too hard into her stirrups. A clue is in the knee which also looks tense. Her feet are too far forward and she reports that she gets numb feet.*

## *Solutions*

- Think about the pressure in your feet, even if your feet do not tend to become numb.
- With your horse at a standstill lift your legs upwards so that your feet lift slightly in the stirrups.
- Lower them gently and aim to let them slowly *sink* down in to the stirrups. Notice that this is quite a different feeling to *pressing* down.

- Alternatively, if you have an assistant ask them to lift each of your legs in turn by cupping their hands under your foot. They should be able to lift each leg relatively easily.
- Raise and lower each leg (with the help of your assistant) aiming to let your leg *relax* down into the stirrup. Your assistant should start to feel the difference and be able to give you feedback.
- Think about this new lighter feeling in your legs and remember it.
- When you think that you have it, work on something else for a while.
- Return to concentrating on the pressure in your feet again and notice if you have reverted back to pressing down too hard.
- Next, ride in a circle and concentrate on relaxing your legs and allowing them to simply 'hang' from your hips.
- If you have an assistant they could take photos to show you the difference in your feet and your knees (your knees will look 'more defined' when you are pressing too hard into the stirrups).
- Keep practising this lesson until it feels 'normal' to have a lighter feeling in your feet and you no longer have to correct them.
- The information in later sections adds to this lesson so don't worry if you cannot get it right just yet.

# 1.3.3: ...feet are not angled correctly

Your feet should *not* be forced to face straight forwards. It is a common misconception that your feet should point straight forwards (or even worse, point inwards!). If you try to do this you will put an unnatural twist on the joints in your legs all the way up to your hips (see picture b in **1.3.2: ...feet are numb**). Pushing (*forcing*) your heels down (rather than allowing them to 'hang' naturally) will also tend to push your feet too far forward *and* turn your toes out (see **4.3.3: ...lower legs are sticking forward** and **4.3.4: ...lower legs are sticking out**.

It is actually quite acceptable to ride with your toes pointing *slightly* out (and even more if disability or previous injury dictates this).

Some people are unable, for one reason or another, to point their toes forward. Trying to force your feet inwards into an unnatural position only causes pain and prevents you from riding well (pain distracts as well as being a sign that something is wrong).

## *Solutions*

- See what happens after you have made adjustments to your leg position resulting in your legs hanging directly underneath you from your hips.

*Typically, once a rider improves their leg position so that their legs hang directly underneath them from their hips, their feet turn out less or not at all. So, see what happens when you have improved your whole leg position.*

## 1.3.4: ...feet are painful

Some people actually curl their toes when riding, usually because they feel tense and insecure and innately they are trying to grip with their feet (a natural human behaviour that occurs due to anxiety).

Just as a stiff, locked jaw results in stiffness far beyond the jaw, tense stiff feet results in stiffness far beyond the feet.

### *Solutions*

- Firstly, if you think your problem is due to confidence you need to address why you feel tense and insecure (see the Horse Rider's Mechanic website article *Your confidence*).
- Turn your attention to your feet and deliberately tense them up even more.
- Then concentrate on relaxing your toes fully and spreading them out in your boots.
- Make sure your footwear allows you to do this comfortably (if not aim to replace your footwear with something more suitable).
- Notice what it feels like when you release the tension and remember the feeling.
- When you think that you have it, work on something else for a while before returning to thinking about how tense your feet are.
- Practice this until the new feeling becomes 'normal'.

For some riders the reason that their feet are painful is because they wear orthotics (foot supports) for walking and their riding boots do not give them the same level of support (even though you are not walking in your boots while riding your feet may still need more support).

## Solutions

- *Experiment* with wearing your orthotics for riding if this is the case. Keep in mind though that some riding boots already have arch support built in so this may not be necessary and may even be detrimental.

A further reason for one or both feet aching is that a rider may have injured their foot or feet in the past. Injuries to the feet are *very* common in horse people due to the delicacy of the human foot compared to the sheer weight of a horse! Most people have had their feet stood by a horse on at some point when first learning where to stand, or not to stand, when around horses.

## Solutions

- *Experiment* with different footwear and/or stirrups. Broader stirrup treads, such as those common in the sport of endurance riding give much more support to your feet. You may also find that strapping your foot (or both feet) helps. More about this in the next section: **Your Ankles**.

*Try experimenting with broader based stirrups if your feet need more support. The stirrups that endurance riders wear are designed to spread the pressure across more of the foot.*

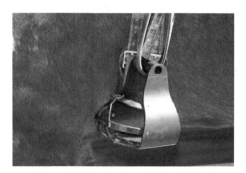

# 1.3.5: ...feet are weighted unevenly

This commonly occurs when a rider has had an injury to one leg which results in an increased stiffness in that leg. For example, a previous injury to an ankle, such as a break, will often result in this particular problem.

It may be that you have not noticed the feeling of uneven pressure in your feet until now but you *have* noticed that you tend to feel better going one way on a circle and unbalanced when going in the other direction. You may also have a tendency to lose one stirrup but not the other.

## Solutions

- Think about the 'history' of your feet and your leg joints and soft tissues (tendons, ligaments). This will give you clues as to where the unevenness might be coming from.
- Address that area of your body when you reach the relevant section of this book.
- Injuries to the feet are mentioned in *1.3.4: ...feet are painful*, but this problem can also occur when there has been a previous injury to any part of the body.

*This rider (right) has an ankle that was injured many years ago and it causes her feet to be weighted unevenly, you can see how one heel drops more than the other. You may need to address a 'problem' area in order to improve the weighting in your feet.*

# 1.3.6: ...feet are losing the stirrups

If a rider 's stirrups move around on their feet or they lose them altogether it can be because they are gripping with their knees (or sometimes the whole length of their legs) in the erroneous belief that this will keep them on their horse.

This problem is a very common self-perpetuating habit that is hard to give up. The gripping may occur because you have stiff joints (and therefore you are not 'engaging' your lower leg properly). Or it could be because you were actually taught to grip (very common). It may also be that you are nervous and you are innately trying to assume the 'foetal position'.

*Gripping with the knees results in 'disengaged' lower legs and insecure stirrups. The problem can originate in various areas of the body or may be due to a lack of confidence. Also it does not help that the myth that you are supposed to grip when riding is still prevalent.*

The 'foetal position' is what your brain tells your body to do when it perceives that you are in danger. It results in you drawing your knees upwards and drawing your hands into your chest. This position curls you into a ball shape and among other things, protects your vital organs when you are in danger. Many riders do this to some degree when they feel insecure without realising they are doing it.

A further problem with this tendency is that it makes a sensitive horse more tense as they feel the gripping pressure from your legs. Also it is the *opposite* of what you need to do to stay on a horse.

In fact, you could say that learning to ride is about learning to do the *opposite* of what your brain tells you to do when you are on a moving object.

Inexperienced riders tend to resort to the 'foetal position' whenever they feel insecure, think about how a beginner will tend to lift their hands and their knees at first, whereas *experienced* riders have usually learned to distribute their weight correctly and keep their centre of gravity (CoG) as *low as possible* in order to ride well. See the Horse Rider's Mechanic website article **Your centre of gravity.**

Even so, experienced riders who lose confidence, despite knowing that they are supposed to 'sit tall', may still revert to this position due to fear (albeit less obviously) if and when it arises.

*Developing as a rider involves learning to do the opposite of what your brain is telling you to do (picture a) and instead distribute your weight correctly (picture b).*

*An experienced rider has also learned that while they should fight the urge to adopt the 'foetal position' whenever mounted on a horse, if they actually fall off then the priority changes. A falling rider should curl themselves up into a ball and attempt to hit the ground rolling. This is preferable to hitting the ground like a spear which is more likely to result in injuries.*

## Solutions

- If you tend to grip, lose your stirrups etc. and you think it may be due to stiff leg joints and 'disengaged' lower legs you will find your solutions when these areas of the body are covered in later sections.
- Make sure you address any confidence issues (see the Horse Rider's Mechanic website article *Your confidence*).
- Work through the rest of this book to improve your position.
- If you are gripping simply because you think you are meant to – you aren't. Allow your legs to simply hang from your hips and 'drape' (more about this in *8: Your lower body*).

*The exercises in Horse Rider's Mechanic Workbook 2: Your Balance are designed to improve your balance and therefore your security. When you have improved your position and balance you will then begin to experience an upward spiral of events rather than the downwards spiral that you may currently be experiencing.*

# 1.3.7: ...feet are letting the stirrup/s twist

In this case the stirrups end up diagonally across the foot or feet (picture a). This may be a habit that has come about from the way a rider was taught and they put the stirrups under their feet in this way thinking that this is how they are meant to be.

Sometimes a rider rides with the stirrups under their toes only (picture b) rather than the balls of their feet. In both cases the feet are not getting enough support.

## Solutions

- Practice putting the treads of the stirrup irons directly across your feet (you may also need to concentrate on weighting the inside of your feet more, see *1.3.1: ...feet are unlevel (from side to side)* and

  practice riding with the stirrups in this new position until it feels 'normal' (it may feel very strange at first).
- Eventually even pressure should be felt right across the balls of your feet and the stirrups should stay in place as you ride, without you having to think about them.
- This problem could also be occurring because you are not weighting your stirrups correctly as described in the previous section.

*By addressing your feet in such detail you may have identified a particular problem that relates to you. You should now have an idea about why it is happening and how to fix it.*

*Don't worry though if you are not able to fix it yet. You may (in fact it is very likely) need to investigate other areas of your body before you can fully solve a problem because a 'problem' body part rarely only affects its immediate area.*

*Remember: aim to work through this book at least twice. Initially in order to identify and start to rectify any problems that you might have. Subsequently, to readdress your issues in light of adjustments that you will have made to other areas of your body.*

*For some riders it will take several sequences of reading, followed by working on a particular problem. Don't worry though because eventually, if you persevere, you will improve your position.*

*Remember: if there is anything you do not understand or need help with after reading this book (or the others in this series) post a question on the Horse Rider's Mechanic Facebook page: www.facebook.com/horseridersmechanic*

*Help is at hand!*

# 2: Your ankles

Your ankles are your major shock absorbing joints when riding. You could call them your 'suspension system'. They work in conjunction with two other very important sets of joints, your knees and your hips.

They should *absorb* the movement of your body and your horse at the same time. They are an interface, if you like, between you and your horse.

'Well behaved' ankles are *crucial* to riding well and for this reason I tend to concentrate on them quite significantly when instructing face to face.

First of all you need to assess the ankles that you have. Ankles tend to fall into one of three groups, 1. too wobbly, 2. just right and 3. too stiff. In fact your joints in general fall into one of these three categories for the purpose of riding so it is a good idea at this stage to think about all of your joints and how they tend to behave.

*Think about how flexible you started out. This will give you vital clues about some of the issues you may be having when riding.*

Everyone tends to become stiffer in their joints as they age and the older you get the more chance there is of previous injuries to add to this stiffness, therefore think about how flexible you were as a child. Were you able to do gymnastics easily (in which case you may be a very loose joint-

25

ed individual)? Did you tend to avoid gymnastics instead, even as a child, (in which case you may be a very stiff jointed individual)? Or maybe you fall somewhere in between?

If you have not read it yet see the Horse Rider's Mechanic website article **Your body**, which has more information about how your body type affects how you ride.

For some people their ankles also differ *from each other,* which means that each ankle may fall into a separate group. This is usually due to previous injuries, but occasionally people have one ankle (or indeed other joint) that naturally behaves differently to its partner. In all cases, each ankle (or other joint) needs to be treated differently.

*Ideal* ankles are not too wobbly *or* too stiff. In fact, this can be said about the rider's body in general, it is about having just the right *balance* between being too wobbly and being too stiff, and ankles are no exception.

## 2.1: Your ankles should...

- Only ever move in an upwards or downwards plane, not a side to side plane.
- Allow you to ride with your heels just below your toes (about 1 to 2 cm or ½ to 1 inch). This should be regarded as the neutral or 'engaged' position.
- Dip and spring when required. They should lower slightly more when weight travels down your legs (if you are rising to the trot or standing in the stirrups for example) and should return to the neutral or 'engaged' position in between.
- Act as shock absorbers, dampening the (mostly upward) movement of your horse and the (mostly downward) movement of you the rider.
- Allow you to ride without pain or fatigue.
- Behave equally. They should both have the same amount of flexibility, or inflexibility.

*Your ankles should only move in the upwards/downwards plane. When they are working correctly they act as shock absorbers, dampening the (mostly upward) movement of your horse and the (mostly downward) movement of you the rider.*

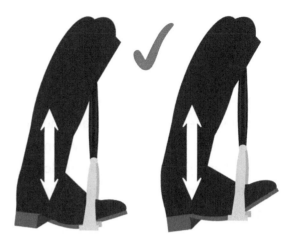

## 2.2: However your ankles may...

- Be too wobbly, (in which case they will tend to 'fall' to the outside) and will be painful, especially in trot.
- Allow your heels to drop too far. This problem is related to having wobbly ankles.
- Be painful (usually on the out-side).
- Be too stiff.
- Be uneven.

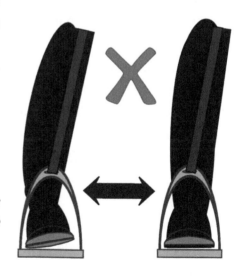

*Your ankles should not move in the side to side plane. If they do this will lead to pain and other problems later on.*

# 2.3: What you can do if...

## 2.3.1: ...ankles are wobbly

Wobbly ankles usually belong to people who have flexible loose joints throughout their body. These are the people who could usually do various gymnastic feats very easily when younger (and often still can when older). These people also tend to love yoga because they are able to achieve the sorts of yoga positions that their stiffer jointed peers can only dream about!

The problem with flexible loose joints is that unless the owner of them stays fit and strong, they are very prone to injury.

A common injury for people with wobbly ankles is spraining an ankle by 'going over' when walking or running on uneven ground. In fact I have yet to meet a rider that has wobbly ankles and has *not* had this happen to them (usually many times).

This leads to lengthened ligaments in their ankle which tend to stay that way (because ligaments do not recover very well once stretched).

When riding with this particular problem the ankles tend to fall to the outside rather than 'dip' and 'spring' as they should in the downwards or upwards plane only.

In addition many riders have been taught to 'wrap' their lower legs around their horse, leading to 'tilted' feet and even pain and numbness in their feet and ankles. Both of these problems were discussed in *1: Your feet.*

When a rider with *stiff* ankles tries to 'wrap' their lower legs around their horse their ankles will simply not bend to the outside, so there is usually no real harm done.

A rider with wobbly ankles however *can* do this and this causes pain and instability in the ankle joint. Because many riders think that a 'no pain no gain' attitude is the best way to go they tend to just get on with it and accept the pain!

## *Solutions*

- If this is your particular problem you will probably benefit from strapping your ankle/s for riding.
- This can be done with an ankle support that can be bought at a pharmacy (picture a).
- Initially try wrapping an equine tail or leg bandage firmly in a figure of eight around your ankle and foot (on the outside of your boot/s - picture b).
- This support does what your own tendons and ligaments would do if they were able.
- You may be very surprised at how much stability this gives your ankles and how much more comfortable riding becomes.
- This support means that you no longer have to concentrate as much to keep your ankles still.
- In some cases wobbly ankles are also painful and strapping them in this way usually alleviates this pain. So an added benefit is that you will no longer be distracted by the pain in your ankles.

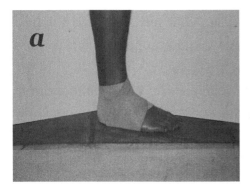

- Once you have supported your ankles, you should no longer feel more stretch on the *outside* of your ankles than the *inside* when rising to the trot or standing in the stirrups.

- Your ankles should now only move up or down, not side to side. In time this will start to feel 'normal' as your brain 'files' this new feeling.
- Check that your inside (the 'big toe' side) of the ball of your foot is being loaded correctly as you are getting used to this new feeling.

*Remember: be cautious about using stirrups that have a tilted stirrup tread (unless you have been advised to by someone such as a medical practitioner who fully understands their effects) as they can make the problem worse and lead to even more ankle problems in time. The tilted bar simply mirrors the incorrect foot angle rather than helps it.*

- You may find that in time your ankles need less support, but in my experience it is easier to loosen a stiff ankle (unless it has been badly injured) than firm up a wobbly ankle (because once ligaments have stretched they tend to stay that way).
- However, just learning how to keep your ankle straight will help enormously so you may manage without support once you are more aware of what your ankles are doing.
- In the longer term, riders with wobbly ankles usually benefit from wearing long boots or at least short boots that lace or zip up firmly around and above the ankles to support them.
- For some riders long boots may be a permanent fixture. Great news if you are just looking for an excuse to have some long boots made to measure!
- If you go the trouble and expense of having long boots made to measure make sure the leather is not *too* soft as it won't give you enough support. Don't forget leather also softens with time and use.

## 2.3.2: ...ankles are too loose

Wobbly ankles can also cause a rider to ride with their heels *too low*.

Again, because riders are usually instructed to ride with their heels *pushed down* a rider with wobbly joints will tend to overdo it and ride with their heels well below their toes. This means that they are *riding with their primary shock absorbers already at full stretch* (picture right).

Think about it, in order for a shock absorber to work it has to be able to move. If it is *already at full stretch* it cannot move any further and therefore cannot absorb any more movement.

Therefore your ankles cannot then dip any further in order to absorb the downward gravitational force on your body as your horse 'bounces' you in trot and canter.

## Solutions

- If this is happening to you, try riding with your feet closer to level. From heel to toe, your heel should only be about 1 to 2cm (½ to almost 1 inch) lower than your toes (picture right).
- It can take a bit of effort to change if you have been riding with your heels jammed down for a while.
- If you have wobbly ankles you should never actually have to *think* about putting your heels down, because they will probably already be too low anyway.
- *Experiment* with different footwear until you get the right amount of support (see the previous section **2.3.1: ...ankles are wobbly**).
- Stirrups that have a very broad tread are great for riders with this problem (picture below) because they support much more of the foot, so seek out this type or endurance stirrups as these tend to be much broader in the tread than conventional stirrups. You may be surprised at how much extra support they give your feet and ankles (see **1.3.4: ...feet are painful**).

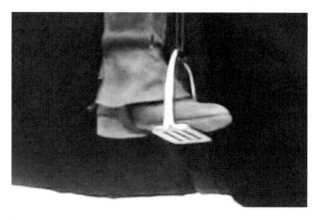

### 2.3.3: ...ankles are painful

If you have wobbly ankles the problem becomes even more apparent when you try to rise to the trot for a period of time, or stand balanced in the stirrups. In this case, a sharp pain is usually felt in the outside of your ankle joints as they are allowed to flex to the outside.

**The second book in this series, Horse Rider's Mechanic Workbook 2: Your Balance, includes lessons that teach you how to improve your balance. Standing in the stirrups in each of the paces (when done correctly), is an excellent way of improving your balance, but you need to make sure your ankles are not too loose or you will experience pain when you stand up.**

### *Solutions*

- Supporting your ankles as described in previous sections should help enormously, but if pain is still felt, the problem may be due to a previous injury.
- Make sure you get any persistent pain checked out by a professional body worker.

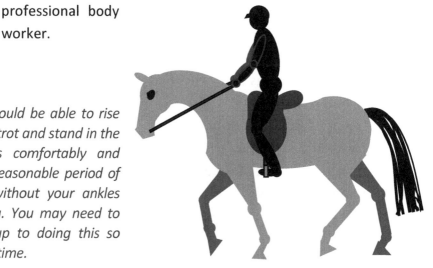

*You should be able to rise to the trot and stand in the stirrups comfortably and for a reasonable period of time without your ankles hurting. You may need to build up to doing this so give it time.*

## 2.3.4: ...ankles are stiff

Some people are just naturally stiffer in their ankle joints than others, and some people have stiffness in one or both ankles due to previous injuries.

People who have naturally stiff ankles will usually have stiffer joints throughout their body in general.

These people also tend to either dislike yoga because they cannot do it, or keep going to yoga thinking that one day they will be able to get their leg behind their head! If this is you, yoga will certainly help to make you more flexible, and you should carry on with this goal rather than thinking that one day you will become a human rubber band!

### *Solutions*

- If you have naturally stiff ankles you may find it helpful to stretch your calves before you mount. You can do this by standing on the edge of a step and letting your heels drop below your toes.

- Then stretch your calves again when you first mount by standing in the stirrups and allowing your weight to pass down your legs and into your heels (picture right).

- If you are stiff in one or both ankles due to old injuries it is advisable to seek professional help, it really is worth the effort as your ankles are crucial to riding well.

- You will benefit from wearing elastic sided short riding boots (that do not restrict your ankle in any way) and half chaps (picture next page) rather than long boots (unless the boots are *very* soft and flexible.

- In time long boots may become an option again if the flexibility of your ankles improves.
- Although there is a limit to how much flexibility will be achieved, on the positive side, stiff joints are generally less prone to injury than looser joints.

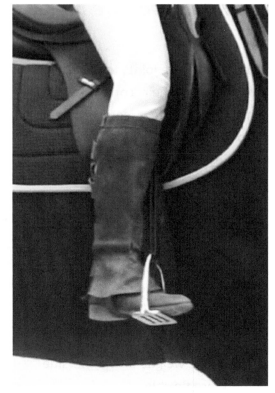

Stiff ankles can also lead to a rider gripping with their knees and losing their stirrups etc. due to the ankle joints not dipping and springing properly.

## *Solutions*

- Practice some standing in the stirrups exercises in walk and trot with a soft knee (no gripping) to engage your lower leg and stretch your calf muscles and Achilles tendons (picture previous page).

**Exercises such as this are covered in the second book in this series, Horse Rider's Mechanic Workbook 2: Your Balance. They particularly work to engage your lower legs.**

- Concentrate on simply 'draping' your legs on your horse rather than hanging on for grim death! (see 8: Your lower body).

## 2.3.5: ...ankles are behaving differently to each other

Some riders have joints that behave differently to their corresponding joint. This is quite a common scenario for all of the joints. In this case the joints need to be treated differently.

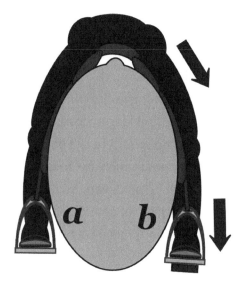

A previously injured joint tends to heal stiffer than before. The picture (right) demonstrates what can happen when a rider has a previously injured ankle joint (a) and a flexible joint that has not been injured (b). The rider will tend to fall to put more weight down the side that is more flexible.

### Solutions

*Picture below, this rider has this situation, a stiff ankle (side a) and a looser ankle (side b). The the looser ankle has been wrapped with a bandage to 'even out' her ankles. Also you could use a broader based stirrup iron on the looser side (it is possible to buy ordinary looking broader based stirrups - see picture in 2.3.2: ...ankles are too loose).*

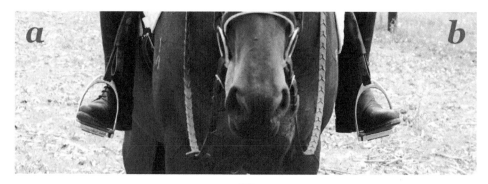

## Case study

*I once taught a man to ride who had previously only ridden 'off road' motorbikes. He picked up how to balance on a horse extremely quickly due to his previous bike riding experience and very high level of confidence. However, he had had a serious ankle injury two years previously (from a motorbike accident), which had left one of his ankles much stiffer than the other.*

*This meant that he tended to keep putting too much weight down his 'good' (uninjured) leg and not enough down his 'bad' (injured) leg.*

*As a consequence the saddle tended to slip to his 'good' side and when working on circles he was particularly unbalanced. He had already had extensive physiotherapy work carried out on his injured ankle so it had almost reached its full potential for recovery (a small amount of further improvement might occur over time but this would probably be offset by stiffness due to age and the injury).*

*In this case I wrapped his 'good' ankle in order to make it firmer so that it behaved more like his 'bad' ankle. This worked very well and he was able to concentrate on the next step in his (horse) riding career.*

**You have now looked at your feet and ankles in great detail. Even if you now feel much better make sure you keep going so that you can 'fine tune' the other parts of your body and end up riding as well as is possible for the benefit of you and your horse.**

# 3: Your calves

The calf muscles are actually a pair of muscles that become the Achilles tendon at the lower end where it joins the heel. The Achilles tendon is the thickest and strongest tendon in the human body. The calf muscles of humans tend to vary a lot. Some people have short thick 'bunched' muscles (which also tend to be strong) and some people have long and usually relatively weaker muscles.

Injuries to calf muscles and Achilles tendons are quite common (not *usually* due to riding, they more often occur during other sporting activities) and these previous injuries can affect a rider.

## 3.1: Your calves should...

- Stabilise your whole lower leg.
- Allow your ankles to dip and spring, by absorbing your downward movement and releasing it in a controlled manner.

## 3.2: However your calves may...

- Be too loose.
- Be too tight.
- Be painful.

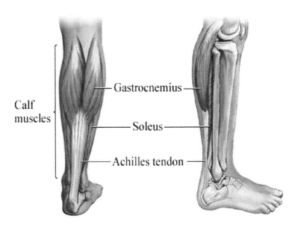

# 3.3: What you can do if…

## 3.3.1: …calves are too loose

Long (looser) calf muscles, per se, are not a problem, but if they are coupled with wobbly ankles they can allow the heels to drop *too* far (see *2.3.1: ..ankles are wobbly*).

### *Solutions*

- Long loose calf muscles need extra support. Now that you understand how to correct a wobbly ankle you should also be able to see how an overly long/loose calf can be helped with some extra support.
- Supporting your ankle *and* calf with firmer riding wear i.e. good quality supportive long boots can help a lot, as can using stirrups with a much wider tread (because they support more of the foot and reduce the amount that the calf can stretch).

## 3.3.2: …calves are too tight

People with short 'bunched' muscles tend to be strong and fast (when fit). They are the sprinters of the human world (akin to a Quarter horse) rather than have endurance (akin to an Arabian horse).

### *Solutions*

- Make sure that your riding wear (i.e. your boots) do not restrict any movement (the opposite to the scenario *3.3.1: …calves are too loose*).
- The information in *2.3.4: …ankles are stiff* also applies here.

### 3.3.3: ...calves are painful

Previous injuries can cause pain in the calves when riding. Returning to riding after a break or learning to ride for the first time will initially cause quite a lot of soreness in the calves.

This is because nothing in every-day life really prepares the calves for the extra stretching that they have to do when you ride a horse. When you ride, your heels 'hang' below your toes and your calves provide elastic energy storage so that they can absorb energy as your body weight travels downwards and then release energy as your body weight travels upwards. So it is not surprising that they may get sore until they become 'riding fit'.

## *Solutions*

- You need to take it slowly if you are not currently riding fit and gauge what is enough for your current condition so that you do not overdo it.
- If you have a history of injury make sure you seek professional help if necessary.
- You may benefit from some stretching exercises before and/or after you mount (see *2.3.4: ...ankles are stiff*).
- Periodically taking your feet out of the stirrups and stretching your toes downwards and circling your feet will help to alleviate sore calves (picture above).

# 4: Your lower legs

Now it is time to look at your lower legs *as a whole*. The first and foremost step in gaining an independent seat (see the Horse Rider's Mechanic website article ***An Independent Seat***) is learning how to stabilise and 'engage' your lower leg (picture right). Without a stable and engaged lower leg your upper body has to compensate by moving around more in order to balance you.

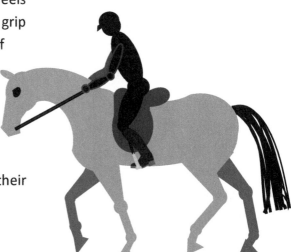

In turn, a not so balanced rider tends to use their lower leg to compensate for any upper body movements (picture lower right). Then, any movements in the upper body are compensated for by moving the lower leg even more.

This becomes a *vicious circle* and causes a rider to become even more unstable. When a rider feels unstable they tend to grip which raises their centre of gravity . This compounds the problem as it makes the rider *even more* unstable and often leads to the rider losing their stirrups as their legs slide upwards.

Instead, a rider with a stable lower leg is almost 'glued' to a horse. It almost sounds too simplistic but if each leg stays down either side of their horse the upper body can move in any direction and the rider will still stay mounted. It is only when a lower leg starts to lift up and away from the side of their horse that a rider starts to become unseated.

An 'engaged' lower leg is able to give leg aids more effectively. Think about how a beginner rider will swing their legs backwards (until they learn otherwise) to 'push their horse on'. This is because their lower leg is not yet developed to the point where they can give a small aid and because they do not yet have an independent seat.

**The third book in this series, Horse Rider's Mechanic Workbook 3: The Aids, will teach you all about how to apply the aids properly.**

We will now look in detail at your lower legs; how they should be positioned and how they should behave.

## 4.1: Your lower legs should...

- Be 'engaged', they should be directly under you, 'primed' and with your ankle slightly flexed.
- Be your 'anchors'.
- Be relatively still.
- Be able to apply the aids (cues/signals) effectively.

## 4.2: However your lower legs may...

- Be 'disengaged'.
- Flap.
- Stick forward.
- Stick out.
- Tilt too far back.
- Be ineffective.

# 4.3: What you can do if...

## 4.3.1: ...lower legs are 'disengaged'

'Disengaged' lower legs means that the lower leg is not in the correct position with the stirrup tread directly across the ball of the foot, heel slightly down, the calf angled back in keeping with the classic ear, shoulder, hip, ankle alignment (more about this in **14: Your body**). So if your lower legs flap, stick forward, stick out or tilt too far back they are 'disengaged' and will be ineffective.

If you have worked through the previous sections you may find that you have already identified your problems in this area, but if you are still having trouble there are a few more things to think about.

*In picture a the riders legs are disengaged. In picture b the lower legs are engaged showing a huge improvement. They are now slightly too far forward but this is partly due to the saddle being forward cut.*

45

## 4.3.2: ...lower legs are flapping

If your lower legs 'flap' it is either because you are making them flap (thinking this is the best way to make your horse move forward), or they are flapping even though you are trying to keep them still.

### *Solutions*

- In the former case you need to be trained how to give the 'go forward' leg aid properly and how to, in turn, train your horse to respond to that aid.
- It is not effective (or fair) to nag away at your horse without receiving a response (your horse will eventually 'switch off' and become 'dead to the leg').

**The correct application of the aids is covered in the third book in this series, Horse Rider's Mechanic Workbook 3: The Aids.**

- If you cannot keep them still despite trying, you need to have another look at your feet, ankles and calves because the problem is probably there.

- Work on some balancing exercises, such as standing in the stirrups with a 'soft' knee (picture right).

**Balance exercises such as this are covered in the second book in this series, Horse Rider's Mechanic Workbook 2: Your Balance. They particularly work to engage your lower leg.**

- If your ankles are stiff you need to concentrate on allowing your heels to gently lower, stretching your calves and Achilles tendons downwards while standing in the stirrups.
- Conversely, if your ankles are wobbly (after giving them some additional support), you need to work on preventing your heels from dropping fully when standing in the stirrups.

### 4.3.3: ...lower legs are sticking forward

You should not be able to see your toes in front of your knees if you glance down. If you can, it is because you are sitting on your horse as you would a chair (hence the term 'chair seat').

*Sitting on a horse as if you are sitting on a chair (picture left) makes a rider much more difficult to carry because a horse's back is weaker the further back it goes. It also makes it difficult for the rider to ride well because they will tend to get left behind the movement. In this picture the rider is not being helped by her saddle which is 'forward cut' (for jumping) and it is 'pulling' her legs forward making it almost impossible for her to sit 'tall'.*

If you sit with your feet too far forward then your weight will tend be too far back in the saddle and you will be sitting on a weaker part of your horse's back.

You will also be behind your horse's centre of gravity, and will therefore get left behind the movement of your horse. See the Horse Rider's Mechanic website article ***Your centre of gravity.***

When you ride a horse you should be sitting and standing (combined) in such a way that if your horse were to disappear in a puff of smoke you would land on your feet in balance. If you ride with a 'chair seat' and your horse disappeared, you would immediately fall on your backside!

*When you ride a horse you should be sitting and standing (combined) in such a way that if your horse were to disappear in a puff of smoke you would land on your feet in balance.*

## *Solutions*

- Occasionally people ride in this position (a 'chair seat') because their saddle makes them more comfortable this way. See the Horse Rider's Mechanic website article ***Your saddle.***
- This position is also common in riders who, despite trying to align their legs underneath themselves properly are also trying (too hard) to push their heels down.
- In this case riders with stiff ankles in particular end up with their feet too far forward (and their toes out) because they cannot do both at the same time.

**Working through the ridden balance exercises in Horse Rider's Mechanic Workbook 2: Your Balance will show you how to achieve a correct balanced position.**

# Case study

*Occasionally a rider has a problem with just one leg rather than both. A rider who came to one of my clinics was having this problem. The offending leg kept shooting forward, especially in trot (picture left). She had had some body work carried out and had no injuries apart from general wear and tear. But because she had been riding like this for many years her muscles had developed in such a way that they were keeping her leg in this position. She knew something was not right but had been unable to fix it.*

*In this case, because she was unable to keep her leg back in the correct position, I tied the stirrup leather with a stretchy bandage to the girth so that she could experience riding without constantly having to keep pulling her leg back underneath her (picture left). Over the course of that day and the next when she returned for a private lesson we were able to remove the bandage and she was able to keep her leg in the correct place and progress further with her riding.*

49

## 4.3.4: ...lower legs are sticking out

This problem is more complex but quite rare. In my experience, it happens when a rider is pushing down into their stirrups too hard (picture right), when they should only be allowing the weight of their legs to 'hang' in their stirrups.

### *Solutions*

- If you think this may be what you are doing you should now notice how hard you are pressing down into the stirrups. Remember, you should only have the weight of your legs going down into the stirrups, which is not the same as actually pressing on them.

- Think about when you stand on the ground, you do not press into the ground you just stand there, you should do the same when mounted.

- Experiment with taking your feet out of the stirrups, letting your legs just 'hang' and then gently placing them back in the stirrups.

- Notice how much pressure you put into the stirrups as you place your feet back in them. Try to make it lighter. Check your stirrup length (see the Horse Rider's Mechanic website article *Your stirrup length*).

- This problem is also seen in riders riding a very sensitive horse when they are afraid to let their legs touch the sides of their horse for fear of upsetting their mount.

- In this case the horse should be trained to accept the riders' legs softly resting against their sides.

### *This subject is covered in detail in Horse Rider's Mechanic Workbook 3: The Aids.*

# 4.3.5: ...lower legs are tilting too far back

This problem is often due to a lack of confidence causing a rider to ride in an 'ejector seat' position. This means that the rider tips forward in their upper body which usually makes their lower legs tip back  (picture right). This position can also lead to back pain as the rider has to use the 'wrong' muscles to balance themselves. The reasons that riders sometimes adopt this position are usually one or both of the following:

- They are trying to keep their weight off of their horse's back thinking this will keep their horse 'happier' and therefore 'safer'.
- So that they can dismount quickly.

## Solutions

- If you identify that this problems is due to a lack of confidence see the Horse Rider's Mechanic website articles **Your confidence, Your safety** and **Your horse**.
- Other reasons for your lower legs tilting backwards are that your ankle joints may be very stiff (already covered) and/or that you have problems with your knees (see **5: Your knees**).
- A further reason can be that your saddle is causing you to tip forwards in your upper body (which in turn causes your lower legs to tip back). See the Horse Rider's Mechanic website article **Your saddle**).

## 4.3.6: ...lower legs are ineffective

You should be able to see by now that if your lower legs are not positioned, weighted and behaving correctly you will have trouble applying effective aids.

If you have been riding a certain way for a long time it will take time to get used to the new feeling as your brain 'files' it and stops trying to get you to go back to your old habits. So don't worry if it takes a bit of time.

Once your new leg position starts to feel less strange you should find that your lower leg is now in a much better position to apply the aids effectively (picture left).

If you were previously riding with your heels up (due to stiff ankles) you will now find that you have to learn to apply a different part of your leg to give an aid (the inside of the lower part of your calf rather than the back of your heel) so this will definitely take time to adjust to. If you have wobbly ankles you will probably not notice as much difference because your heels would have been down anyway and you should already have been using the correct part of your leg to apply the aid.

**The correct application of the aids is covered in the third book in this series, Horse Rider's Mechanic Workbook 3: The Aids.**

# 4.4: Your lower legs - a recap

Improving your lower legs involves:

- Identifying any problems.
- Taking the appropriate steps such as wearing gear that allows your ankles to move more freely (in the case of stiff ankles) or supporting wobbly ankles with strapping and/or better boots. You may even want to consider experimenting with stirrups that support a larger area of your feet.
- Checking your stirrup length and taking them up if necessary (it often is!). This is covered in more detail in **6: Your thighs**
- Placing your feet in the stirrups correctly, weighting all of the ball of your foot, not just the outside, then working through balance exercises (standing in the stirrups with a soft knee, see the book *Horse Rider's Mechanic Workbook 2: Your Balance*) to get your ankles working properly in a downwards/upwards plane only.
- All of this leads to proper engagement of your lower legs (picture above).

*Remember: if there is anything you do not understand or need help with after reading this book (or the others in this series) post a question on the Horse Rider's Mechanic Facebook page:*
*www.facebook.com/horseridersmechanic*

# 5: Your knees

The knees are part of the trilogy of leg joints that a rider relies on to ride well. The knee joint (patella) is one of the most intricate joints in the human body. It is a complex pivotal hinge joint that connects the bones in the upper and lower leg.

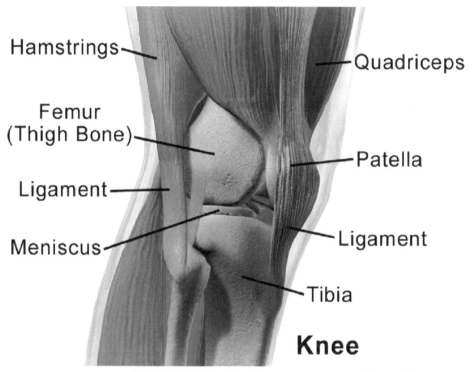

Source: www.commons.wikimedia.org

*The human knee is a highly complex joint. It is also one of the hardest working joints in the body.*

Problems with a rider's knees commonly occur due to previous injuries (in one or both knees). As people age, the chances of having old injuries that affect them is high, as is plain 'wear and tear' to their knees.

Many mature adults these days have had knee operations, including full knee 'reconstructions'. In my experience correct riding seems to be very good for 'problem' knees.

The most common problem with riders in terms of what they think they should be doing with their knees when riding is that they have usually been told to grip with them. Gripping with the knees is incorrect.

## 5.1: Your knees should...

- Touch the saddle but not grip. In fact your whole leg should 'drape' around your horse without any more inward pressure than what is required to keep your leg still (unless giving an aid).
- Open and close without pain.
- Be strong enough to cope with concussion absorption and flexion.

## 5.2: However your knees may...

- Grip.
- Flap.
- Be painful.
- Be weak.
- Be stiff.

*The whole length of your legs should 'drape' around your horse without any more inward pressure than what is required to keep them still. Another way of thinking about it is that your legs should simply 'hang' from your hips when they are not being utilised to give the aids.*

*Because this rider is gripping with her knees, the weight that should be travelling downwards is instead travelling upwards. Raising the centre of gravity in this way makes a rider very insecure indeed.*

## 5.3: What you can do if...

### 5.3.1: ...knees are gripping

There is a whole world of difference between having enough tension in the muscles of the legs to keep the knees still and actually gripping inwards with the knees. Any actual gripping causes your weight, which should travel downwards and be absorbed into the shock absorbing mechanism of your lower legs, to stop at that point (the knees) . Therefore the kinetic energy that *should* travel downwards and be dispersed, instead pops you upwards out of the saddle. This leads to you feeling even more insecure, gripping even harder, resulting in 'disengagement' of the lower legs. You may also lose your stirrups too.

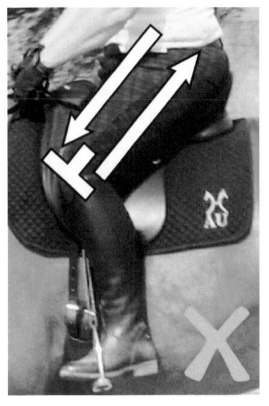

Gripping with your knees creates a vicious circle of events. Your weight should be travelling downwards all the way to your ankles and feet. This keeps your centre of gravity low and ultimately keeps you on the horse. When you grip with your knees your weight stops travelling downwards at that point (your knees) and this means that your weight then travels upwards instead of downwards. Your ankles in particular are then prevented from doing their job, of absorbing that downwards force. This causes you to feel insecure which usually results in you to gripping even harder!

## Solutions

- If this is happening, you need to concentrate on releasing the inward gripping pressure.
- Experiment with just how much muscle tension is needed to keep your knees still but also allows weight to travel all the way down your legs.
- Try the following exercise. Initially stiffen your knees and deliberately grip (make sure you are not upsetting your horse by doing this, if you are, stop doing it). Notice how difficult riding becomes.
- Now concentrate on releasing that inwards pressure, to the point that your legs feel quite loose.

*In this cross section (picture right) you can see how gripping causes your weight to travel upwards instead of downwards*

- Now increase the pressure in small increments until it feels just right and your knees stay relatively still.
- Experimenting in this way teaches you to really *think* about what your body is doing. It also gives you the skills to apply this method to other parts of your body whenever necessary in the future.

## 5.3.2: ...knees are flapping

The opposite of gripping knees, this problem usually occurs in canter as the 'rolling' movement causes the knees to keep leaving the saddle.

### Solutions

- In this case concentrate on 'firming up' the tension in your leg muscles until you can keep them still.
- If your lower leg is disengaged your knees are more likely to flap so make sure you work to improve the engagement of your lower legs.
- Carry out the same exercise as described in the previous section *5.3.1: ...knees are gripping,* until you have the right amount of inward pressure to keep your knees still (without gripping).
- As with other problems flapping knees are often just a result of other areas of the body 'not working properly.' So think about where the problem could be originating.

### 5.3.3: ...knees are painful, weak or stiff

Stiffness is usually due to previous injuries and/or 'wear and tear'. As already mentioned 'wear and tear' of the knees is very common in mature people, added to the fact that many sports are notorious for injuring the knees. Riding itself does not usually cause knee injuries but dismounting incorrectly is a very common cause of knee injuries.

## *Solutions*

- Aiming to ride reasonably regularly is better than leaving it too long between rides.
- Weak knees need support, at least initially (when returning to riding or first learning to ride). However correct riding is usually very good for the knee joints.
- It is possible to buy a specialist knee brace for riders (picture below) from a saddlery store or via the Internet. Sports shops and pharmacies usually sell them too (although not specific riding knee supports they work in the same way).

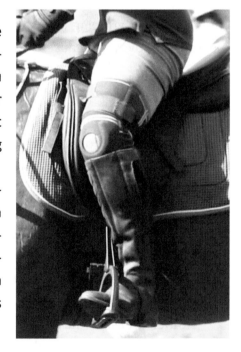

- Pain in the knees is usually due to stiffness and/or previous injury so it may improve as you become more riding fit. Never ignore pain though, if it is not improving with regular riding seek professional help.
- Be *very* careful when dismounting if you have problem knees. In fact you should be always be careful because dismounting incorrectly is a common cause of knee injuries in riders.

*I have met many riders that have injured their knees when dismounting because they jumped off their horse too quickly, landing too hard and with their legs too straight. Another common injury is to land and then slip under the horse. Your knees should always be bent as you land. More mature riders should not fling themselves off at the same speed that many younger riders can. You may need help with dismounting at first (or possibly long term).*

# 6: Your thighs

Your thighs have very strong and relatively long muscles (compared to the rest of your body).

These muscles have to work hard when you are rising to the trot or cantering. They get particularly tired if you are returning to riding or learning to ride as an adult. They do however quickly strengthen so the discomfort is usually short lived.

Ideally a rider should have long, rather than bulky, thigh muscles, but of course this is only the ideal.

Many people have bulk in the thigh area (either fat or muscle or both) that can work against them because it gets in the way (muscle is great but if you have the legs of a body builder for example that muscle is superfluous).

Heavy legs are better than a heavy top half (not that you usually have a choice!) because then your centre of gravity is lower (see the Horse Rider's Mechanic website articles *Your centre of gravity* and *Your body*).

Many riders ride with stirrups that are *too* long thinking that this will give them the 'long legs' that they so desire! (picture right). But all this does is make it impossible for them to utilise the dip and spring action of the leg joints properly (see the Horse Rider's Mechanic website article *Your stirrup length*).

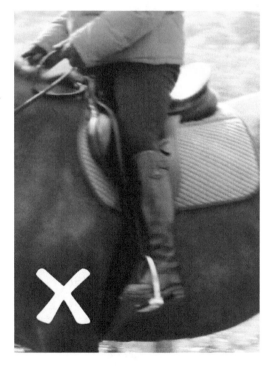

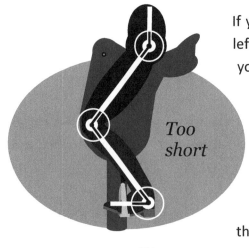

**Too short**

If your stirrups are too short (picture left). You will have too much bend in your leg joints and you will tend to tire more quickly.

On the other hand, if your stirrups are too long (picture middle) you will find it difficult to rise to the trot properly because in order to stand up in their stirrups your heels will have to come *upwards* so that your seat can clear the saddle. So at that moment in time you will be standing on 'tip toe'.

**Too long**

The correct stirrup length (picture below) helps you to ride as well as possible by having just the right amount of bend in the joints. So in light of what you have learned so far review the length of your stirrups and experiment with different lengths.

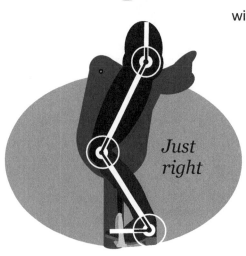

**Just right**

*The balance exercises in Horse Rider's Mechanic Workbook 2: Your Balance help you to establish the correct stirrup length.*

# 6.1: Your thighs should...

- Lay still against the saddle without gripping.
- Particularly work to help you rise to the trot efficiently, stand balanced in the stirrups (when necessary) and canter comfortably.
- Assist in giving a leg aid (the correct application of the aids is covered in the third book in this series, **Horse Rider's Mechanic Workbook 3: The Aids**).
- Be at the correct angle for effective riding. The stirrups of an experienced rider can be *slightly* longer than those of an inexperienced rider but they still should allow the rider to rise up and forward out of the saddle with ease without the heel rising as they do so.

# 6.2: However your thighs may...

- Grip.
- Flap.
- Be painful.
- Be weak.

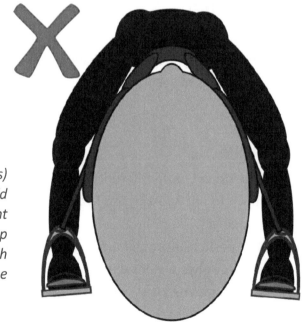

*Your thighs (and knees) should not flap. You should have just the right amount of muscle tension to keep them still but not to push you upwards out of the saddle.*

# 6.3: What you can do if...

## 6.3.1: ...thighs are gripping

Gripping thighs cause a rider to raise their centre of gravity (see the Horse Rider's Mechanic website article *Your centre of gravity*). It is a similar (and usually connected) problem to knees that grip and therefore the solution in that case is the same (see *5.3.1: ...knees are gripping*).

### Solutions

- Increase the tension in your thighs and then relax them.
- Notice what it feels like when they are relaxed.
- This is the feeling you should be aiming for.

However the gripping in your thighs may be because you have tightness in your hips that needs investigating. See *7: Your hips* for more information.

## 6.3.2: ...thighs are flapping

Again similar and connected to the same problems with knees (see *5.3.2: ...knees are flapping*). You should have just the right amount of muscle tension in your thighs to keep them still but not to push you upwards out of the saddle.

### Solutions

- Experiment with different amounts of inwards pressure (from too much to not enough) until you are able to keep them still, without gripping.
- This particular problem, along with flapping knees, usually sorts itself out once a rider corrects their leg position as a whole so see what happens after you have looked at the various areas of your body in detail and have made any necessary adjustments.
- Different types of saddles also help or hinder this problem so see the Horse Rider's Mechanic website article *Your saddle*).

### 6.3.3: ...thighs are painful or are weak

This is usually due to undeveloped muscles and will generally no longer be a problem once you are fully 'riding fit'.

As a side, even if someone is very fit due to some other form of exercise (e.g. running), they will not automatically be 'riding fit' when they first begin to ride. All activities use muscles in different ways so some soreness, especially in the thigh (and calf) muscles, is to be expected when first learning to ride or returning to riding after a break.

Just the same as for other aches and pains though, weigh up what is reasonable and monitor any soreness. If you are concerned then seek professional help.

## *Solutions*

- Aim to ride as regularly as possible but keep the sessions short.
- If you get very sore while riding you will tend to become more tense when you actually need to relax more.

- Even if you are riding in a lesson or as part of a clinic do not be afraid to ask if you can stop for a few minutes and stretch your legs out (picture right) or even dismount for a few minutes for a change of position for your legs.
- Then when you remount, concentrate on relaxing your thighs and letting your legs simply 'hang' from your hips.

# 7: Your hips

Your hips are the third set of joints involved in the shock absorbing mechanism of your legs and play a very important role in riding correctly.

Like knees, hips do not tend to age well in the human body and most people have some 'wear and tear' by a certain age. The hip joints also commonly suffer from injuries (both from riding accidents and from 'everyday life' such as sporting injuries etc.).

So it stands to reason that many riders have a problem with this area of their body and when they do it can show up as 'crookedness'.

Riding *correctly* can be very beneficial for this part of the body but if you are concerned about anything seek professional help.

## Pelvis and hips

1. Right ilium
2. Sacrum
3. Sacroiliac joint
4. Left ilium
5. Coccyx
6. Pubis
7. Ischium
8. Pubic symphysis
9. Femoral/hip joint

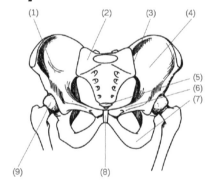

Source: www./commons.wikimedia.org

## 7.1: Your hips should...

- Be able to *follow* the complex movements of your horse's back, this is relatively easy in walk and rising trot but more complicated in sitting trot and canter.
- Allow your legs to 'hang' from them comfortably.
- Stay evenly across your horse's back (picture next page).
- Allow equal pressure to travel to each seat bone.

## 7.2: However your hips may...

- Be painful or stiff and therefore unable to follow the complex movements of your horse's back.
- Be crooked and cause you to ride unevenly.

## 7.3: What you can do if...

### 7.3.1: ...hips are painful or are stiff

Apart from injuries or 'wear and tear' to the hip joint itself this problem is usually down to not enough flexibility in the soft tissues around the hip.

In particular many people are tight in the ligaments and tendons that run from the hip area down towards the *front* of the thigh. When a rider gets on a horse they are often asking those soft tissues to do the *opposite* of what they are comfortable doing. Especially if their day job involves lots of sitting in a chair. Sitting allows those soft tissues to stay short and un stretched. Riding (and to some extent walking) stretches them.

The hip joint may even 'cramp' simply because these soft tissues are 'out of their comfort zone'.

### *Solutions*

- You may benefit from some stretching exercises before mounting in which case 'lunges' may be useful (picture right).
- Once you are mounted you can stretch your legs down and back several times *before* you put your feet in the stirrups.

70

- While your legs are stretched down, raise and lower your toes to stretch the backs of your legs (picture right).

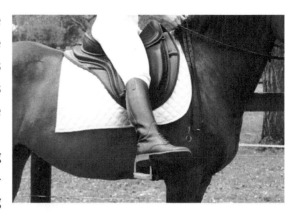

- You could also bring your legs up and forward while stretching in this way to relieve tight soft tissues in the hips.

- Lifting your legs up like this (picture right) is also a useful way of locating your seat bones. You will feel them as soon as both of your thighs lift off the saddle.

- If you are particularly tight in the hips you may need to stop for a break several times while riding and do these stretches.

- Dismounting and walking for a while can help too (plus this will give your horse's back a rest!).

- Investigate your saddle to check that it is helping rather than hindering you. The width of the 'twist' of a saddle is particularly important for people with 'problem' hips. This is the part of the saddle that sits directly under the seat bones (picture next page), some saddles are wide and some narrow in the twist. A narrow twist is not necessarily better (see the Horse Rider's Mechanic website article *Your saddle*).

*The 'twist' of a saddle*

- Even the width and movement of your horse may make a difference and unfortunately some horse/rider combinations just do not work if a rider has particularly serious problems with their hips. (see the Horse Rider's Mechanic website article *Your horse*). Even if you have wide hips it may be that due to injury and/or 'wear and tear' you are no longer able to ride comfortably in a certain saddle, or on a very wide horse or a horse that does not have smooth movement.

*Remember: problems with the hips will often prevent a rider from being able to follow the complex movements of their horse's back properly.*

*This is covered in detail in Horse Rider's Mechanic Workbook 2: Your Balance. So aim to get help if necessary, look at your saddle and your horse in detail and then work on straightening yourself as much as is possible by improving your position and balance.*

# 7.3.2: ...hips are crooked

When a rider's hips are crooked this crookedness is usually also seen as 'legs behaving badly'.

This crookedness may be originating in the pelvis or torso. Therefore the upper body may behave badly too.

Think about which side of your body is the strongest and which is the weakest. Some people are reasonably ambidextrous while others are very right or left handed.

Look at how you tend to stand when you are not trying to stand straight (standing relaxed). If you tend to stand with one side of your waist collapsed then you are likely to do this when mounted too.

The side that collapses will tend to slide towards the middle of the saddle. The leg on the collapsed side will tend to 'ride up' *and* lose the stirrup more often (picture above right).

## *I cannot stress enough that if you are concerned about irregularities in your body then you should seek professional help.*

## *Solutions*

- When you have done all you can to rectify the problem unmounted you will need to teach your body to ride straighter. The reason I say 'straighter' rather than 'straight' is that some people may never be able to be totally straight due to the nature of their problem. In fact *no one* will ever be totally straight, it is just a matter of degrees. If your crookedness is due to a serious injury/disability you may never be able to ride even close to straight.

- It is a good idea though to aim to make yourself as *easy as possible* for your horse to carry.
- In this case ensure that your horse is fit enough and strong enough to deal with a particularly unbalanced rider (see the Horse Rider's Mechanic website articles **Your body** and **Your horse**).
- It will take time to re-educate your body. If you have been riding crooked for any length of time it will feel 'odd' to sit straight, even though mirrors, your assistant, photographs and video's all tell you differently.
- Even if you have undergone 'straightening' with a human body worker you may still feel odd when you ride again because your muscles and other soft tissues have to 'learn' a new way of operating.
- This is an area where it really helps to have an assistant (see the Horse Rider's Mechanic website article **Your assistant**). See if you can arrange to have someone watch you, even if you normally ride alone.
- Your assistant can place you in the correct position or at least describe which parts of you need to move where, then walk behind you (at a safe distance) and tell you if you are remaining straight. They can also take photos etc. which help because then you will be able to see what they see.
- Make sure you wear clothing that enables your assistant to see if you are straight or not (i.e. avoid wearing a baggy top).
- Have your saddle checked if you have been riding crooked for some time as that may have become more compacted on one side than the other.
- Once your hips are positioned correctly relax and let your seat be moved by your horse's back.

*This is covered in detail in the chapter* Riding the walk *in the second book in this series, Horse Rider's Mechanic Workbook 2: Your Balance, but for now aim to stop any pushing or shoving with your seat and let your legs simply 'hang' from your hips.*

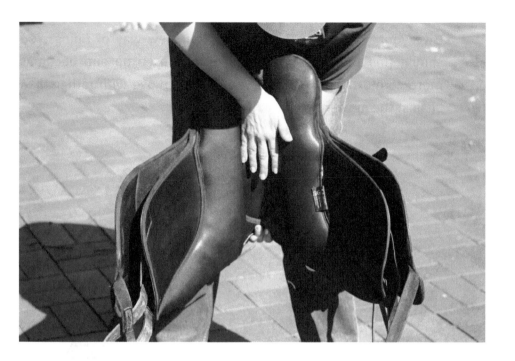

*A professional saddle fitter should have a look at your saddle if you have been riding crooked for some time as it may have become more compacted on one side than the other.*

- Concentrate on the feeling in both seat bones and think about whether you have equal weight in them.
- If you have trouble feeling your seat bones stop your horse, take your feet out of your stirrups and lift both knees upwards (see picture of rider doing this in *7.3.1: ...hips are painful or are stiff*) you should immediately feel both seat bones. Concentrate on continuing to feel them as you lower your legs again and put your feet back in the stirrups.
- You will need to keep mentally checking this area until it becomes 'ingrained' and you can maintain more equal pressure. It will take time for your brain to 'file' this new feeling so don't rush and don't move on to faster paces until you can keep your hips relatively even.

- Give your horse time to adjust to your new way of riding. You should find that your horse begins to loosen up and becomes more comfortable to ride as you start to move *with* rather than against the movement.

*The centrifugal force*

- When you do move on to faster paces on a circle the centrifugal force (the same thing that happens to your clothes in the washing machine on the spin cycle, picture above) causes your hips to slide to the outside. You need to concentrate on stretching down your inside leg to counteract this force.
- This is very important and once you have mastered it you will no longer lose your inside stirrup in trot or canter if this was occurring before.

- Try the following exercise that helps to improve crookedness in the upper body. Place a stick or riding whip under your thumbs and walk/trot with it in place. You will come across this exercise again later in *12: Your hands*. By riding with a stick under your thumbs your body has to straighten in order to rise properly in rising trot (picture below). Many riders are surprised as their core muscles have to work harder (because their hands can no longer 'help' them to rise by moving). Often this movement has been so slight the rider has been totally unaware of it. The stick exercise sorts it out and re-educates the core muscles to work more evenly.

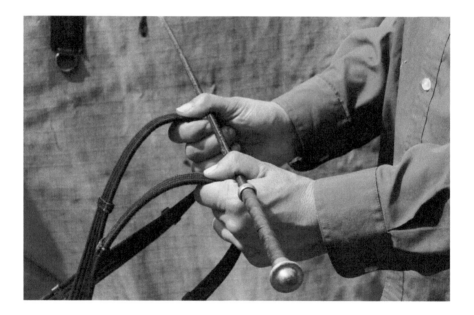

# 8: Your lower body

This section looks at your lower body *as a whole*. It is a recap of the previous sections *and* has some further information.

## 8.1: Your lower body should...

- *Follow* the movement of your horse's back. This enables your horse to move forward unhindered *and* allows you to absorb the movement that is generated by your horse into your hips, knees and ankles.

- 'Hang' from your hips down either side of your horse, with the weight of your legs going down to your feet. A good rider sits/stands across a horse (picture right). Riding is combining the two (see the Horse Rider's Mechanic website article *Do you sit or stand?*).

- Be responsible for giving the 'go faster' aids and for positioning the 'back half' of your horse. Your leg aids *increase* your horse's speed when applied together and move your horse's hindquarters sideways when required; this is covered in detail in *Horse Rider's Mechanic Workbook 3: The Aids*.

*A good rider both sits and stands across a horse.*

## 8.2: However your lower body may...

- Be unable to follow and absorb the movement.
- Be unable to maintain position.
- Be unable to give the aids effectively.

# 8.3: What you can do if...

## 8.3.1: ...lower body is unable to follow and absorb the movement

'Old habits die hard' is a very apt saying. By now if you have made adjustments to the position of your whole *lower body* it should just be a matter of training yourself to allow your lower body to *follow* the movement of your horse's back. Likewise, if the joints of your legs are in the correct position, they are set up to better absorb the movement that is generated by your horse. Simply placing yourself in the correct position though is not the whole solution. You also have to improve your balance which will in turn improve the security of your seat.

### *Solutions*

- Think about relaxing and *letting your horse move you* rather than the other way round. This can be difficult if you have been riding 'with the brakes on' (still and stiff) or 'shoving' with your seat in an effort to keep your horse moving.
- You also need to learn how to absorb the (mainly) upwards and downwards movement of your horse into your leg joints as efficiently as possible. If you are still having trouble doing this the subject is covered in detail in *Horse Rider's Mechanic Workbook 2: Your Balance*.

## 8.3.2: ...lower body is unable to maintain position

Remember, your legs should be relatively still and directly under you (in such a position that if your horse was to disappear, you would land on the ground, with your knees slightly bent, without falling forwards or backwards). This is part of the classic ear, shoulder, hip, ankle alignment which is *essential* for good balance and makes a *huge* difference to how you ride *and* how much easier it is for your horse to carry you.

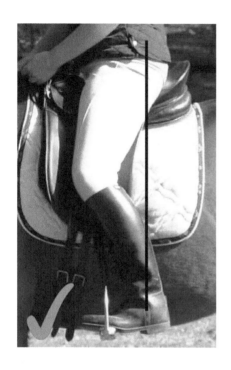 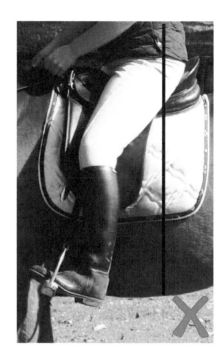

If you cannot maintain this position it is usually because you are either:

- prevented from doing so by your saddle,
- prevented from doing so by your anatomy,
- both of the above.

## Solutions

- If you still have a problem with maintaining position you need to start examining *why* in more detail. A rider *should* be able to keep their leg 'down and back' (rather than forward as in a 'chair seat').
- A good modern dressage saddle will help you to keep your leg in the correct position but, because it will stretch your thighs down and back, it may also feel quite uncomfortable at first (because you are stretching soft tissues that are not used to being stretched).
- If you are not yet 'riding fit' try not to make any hasty decisions about choosing a particular type of saddle while you are going through this stage (see the Horse Rider's Mechanic website article **Your saddle**).

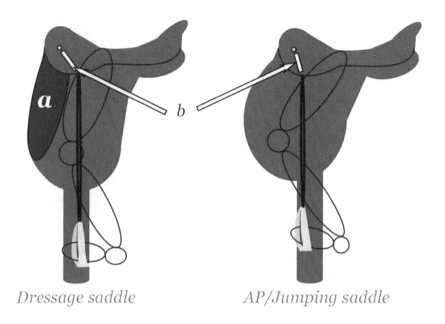

*Dressage saddle*  *AP/Jumping saddle*

*A Dressage Saddle helps you to keep your legs in the correct position by supporting your thigh (a) and by having the stirrup bar positioned further back than it is on an All Purpose (AP) or Jumping Saddle (b).*

- Usually this area (the soft tissues around the hips etc.) will feel more comfortable with frequent riding as long as you continue to maintain your leg in the correct position (but do not overdo it at first, see *7.3.1: ...hips are painful or are stiff*).
- It is normal to feel sore in this area when first returning to riding after a break but not normal to feel sore when riding regularly.
- Any persistent pain should be investigated by a professional.
- At the same time as keeping your legs down and back your legs should simply 'drape' down the sides of your horse. Think about how curtains 'drape'. They don't cling to the window or lift themselves away from the window. Your legs should 'drape' in the same way.
- The mounted exercises in *Horse Rider's Mechanic Workbook 2: Your Balance* 'train' your legs to stay underneath you. These exer-

cises teach your body to balance properly so that riding any other way is actually counterproductive.

- When you are in balance you will use less energy to ride and your horse will be able to carry you much more easily.

# 8.4: Your lower body – a recap

Your lower body is responsible for giving the 'go faster' (speed up) aids *and* for positioning the 'back half' of your horse i.e. for moving the hindquarters sideways (lateral movements). This is all covered in detail in *Horse Rider's Mechanic Workbook 3: The Aids.*

At this stage your aim should be to position yourself as well as possible so that you can work through the balance exercises in *Horse Rider's Mechanic Workbook 2: Your Balance.*

Then your flexibility (if you were stiff), your riding fitness (if you were unfit) and your stability (if you had poor balance) will all have improved.

This will lead to clearer more concise aids. So, improving your lower body involves:

- Identifying any problems.
- Checking that your lower legs are properly 'engaged'.
- Making sure that your knees and thighs are not gripping, flapping or behaving badly in general.
- Making sure that your legs 'hang' from your hips and that your seat bones are weighted equally on the saddle.
- Checking that your gear (this includes your own riding gear and your horse's gear) helps you to ride well rather than hinders you.

**Remember: if there is anything you do not understand or need help with after reading this book (or the others in this series) post a question on the Horse Rider's Mechanic Facebook page:**
**www.facebook.com/horseridersmechanic**

# 9: Your torso

Your torso is your upper body not including your arms or head. Men tend to be longer (proportionately) in the torso than women (pictures below left and right respectively). This means that some women have an advantage due to their centre of gravity being lower when riding a horse (See the Horse Rider's Mechanic website articles *Your centre of gravity* and *Your body*).

A strong upper body (in terms of possessing 'core strength') helps enormously in the quest to be a better rider. But just as with other areas of your body, it takes time to strengthen this area. Riding (well) is one of the best ways to strengthen your torso.

The conformation of the lower back varies from rider to rider as does the human body in general.

The information that is readily available about what your lower back should be doing when riding does not usually take account of the fact

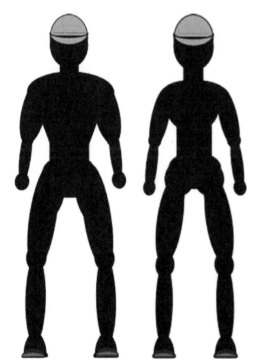

that everyone is built differently. You should *aim* to have only a small curve (inwards) in your lower back.

Some people have a condition which may hinder this somewhat such as lordosis (or 'sway back') where their lower back is very curved inwards, or kyphosis (rounded back) where their upper back is (overly) rounded outwards. Other people have a certain amount of scoliosis (spine curvature to the side) as well as lordosis and/or kyphosis.

The good news is that people of all shapes and sizes, including those with actual 'disabilities', still manage to ride well.

Having a 'perfect' body (if such a thing exists) is only one factor that helps a rider to ride well. There are other far more important factors that help a rider. See the Horse Rider's Mechanic website article Your attitude.

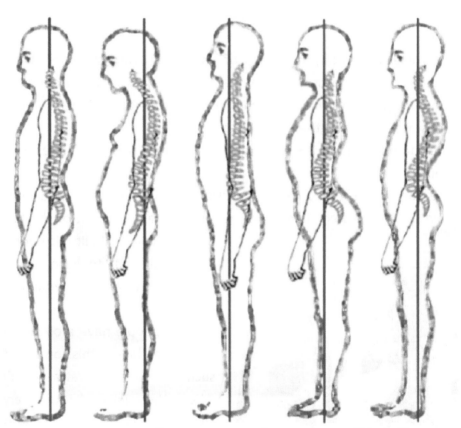

*Source: www./commons.wikimedia.org*

*The picture (above) shows variations from the 'norm' in the human spine. Starting with 'normal' on the left, then kyphosis (rounded upper back), too straight (not enough curvature), lordosis (very curved inwards) and then kyphosis and lordosis together. Other people have a certain amount of scoliosis (spine curvature to the side) as well as lordosis and/or kyphosis.*

# 9.1: Your torso should...

- Give the illusion of stillness (while actually absorbing movement through your lower back).
- Mirror the angle of your horse's shoulders.
- Be positioned equally over the back of your horse (picture right).
- Have vertical (perpendicular to the ground) as a neutral position and keep this vertical position, even when your horse is travelling uphill or downhill.
- Have only a small curve in the lower back.
- Be strong enough to ride comfortably.

# 9.2: However your torso may...

- Move excessively (wobble in the middle).
- Be crooked.
- Slouch.
- Tip forward.
- Lean back.
- Be too arched in the lower back.
- Be painful (usually lower back pain).

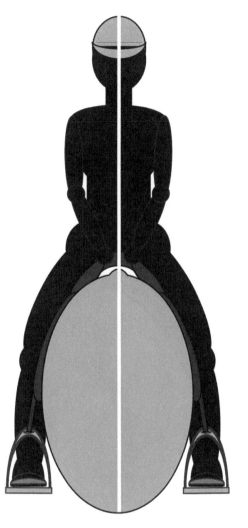

# 9.3: What you can do if...

## 9.3.1: ...torso is moving excessively

This is usually seen in riders (often dressage riders) that are riding big moving horses in extended (sitting) trot (picture below) and sometimes in canter too.

If they are not absorbing the movement correctly into their hips, knees and ankles the kinetic energy goes upwards rather than downwards (it has to go somewhere). In some riders excessive movement of the head is also seen.

### Solutions

- For excessive upper body and head movement (in sitting trot and canter) you need to work on improving absorption of your horse's movement through your ankles, knees and hips. This involves allowing the weight from your hips *downwards* to travel down and into your leg joints.

- In many cases the stirrups are too long and this prevents the correct use of these leg joints (see the Horse Rider's Mechanic website article *Your stirrup length*).

**There is also a whole chapter devoted each to sitting trot and canter in Horse Rider's Mechanic Workbook 2: Your Balance: It covers in detail how to absorb the movement correctly in these gaits.**

- Once you have improved your ability to absorb the movement of your horse through your lower body you can practice 'sitting taller' through your torso.
- You need to perfect this in sitting trot and then you can apply what you have learned to canter.
- Aim to lift your sternum (breast bone) without stiffening your back. If you feel yourself starting to bounce go back to concentrating on your lower body and check that you are absorbing the movement correctly down through your legs to your feet. *Only then* switch to thinking about your upper body again.
- Keep doing this until you can stretch downwards through your lower body *and* simultaneously stretch upwards through your upper body.
- This is not easy but once you have accomplished it you will be nearer to obtaining an independent seat.

## 9.3.2: ...torso is crooked

Crookedness through the torso is very common. In fact we *all* have asymmetry to some degree in our bodies so for most people it is just a matter of to what degree. For some people it is a physical 'abnormality' and there will be a limit to how much improvement can be achieved. Others may not have any real straightness issues but instead have poor posture. In this case quite significant improvement may occur if the rider is made aware of it and they are willing to work to improve their posture.

Riding is excellent for improving crookedness but it would be wrong of me to say that we should all be perfectly straight. For some people this is just not possible.

*Initially the rider in this picture (above) does not look too crooked but when straight lines are placed on the same picture you can see that there is some asymmetry.*

Therefore we should *aim* to make ourselves as symmetrical as possible (for our sake and that of our horse) and the suggestions in this section will certainly help. As always, seek professional help if necessary. Crookedness in the upper body is often linked to a rider having hips that are crooked.

As an example, a person that I taught that had had a very serious back injury many years ago. His crookedness is now also in his hips and pelvis and all the way down both legs. One of his calves is narrower (by about 2cm (1 inch) on the same side of his body as his original injury. So even though his original injury was not in his hips, pelvis or legs they are now just as affected as if they had been injured. See **7.3.2: ...hips are crooked**.

## *Solutions*

- When it comes to straightening up this area of the body (after you have done all you can to straighten your body while unmounted), I usually recommend riding in a back support at least for a while.

- The back support can be placed so that you become aware when you are starting to collapse on one side (picture right). For example if you fit it so that the padded section is on  the side that tends to collapse you will feel when it starts to happen.

- Again, having an assistant is very useful for such a serious problem. If possible you need someone to sit or stand where they can see and let you know when you are starting to collapse on one side.

- Try riding with your arm in the air above your head to stretch the side of your body that tends to collapse (picture a next page).

- Try riding with the back of your hand in the small of your back to realign a shoulder that tends to be too far forward (picture b next page).

- Crookedness does not always show up as being collapsed on one side. It may be that you twist more to one side than the other, but your shoulders stay almost level.

- This will be noticed especially when you ride a circle. You will be comfortable in one direction and your torso will be able to mirror the angle of your horse's shoulders around the corner, but in the other direction your shoulders will be angled one way (to the outside) while those of your horse are angled the other (to the inside).
- Your assistant (when standing in the middle of the circle as you ride around them) should be able to see this.
- Think about your chest as having eyes and that those eyes need to be able to 'look' around the circle to see where you are going. You should not need to exaggerate this however on your 'bad' side you may need to deliberately keep your outside shoulder forward until your brain accepts the new feeling.
- Your assistant can simply use the key word 'eyes' as you ride around them to remind you.

### 9.3.3: ...torso is slouching

Rounded shoulders (picture right) are usually seen in people that also have poor posture when standing, walking or sitting on a chair. Likewise people who have good posture *off* a horse will tend to have good posture when riding, so think about what *you tend* to do when unmounted.

This is an area that you can easily work to improve in your everyday life (by practising standing, walking and sitting better). Most of us have a tendency to slouch because most of us spend too much time sitting, usually in a badly designed chair.

Even a well designed chair may still result in you sitting slouched. Standing up frequently is one of the best ways of alleviating the problems of too much sitting, so if you work in an office make sure you find as many reasons as possible to stand up and walk on a regular basis.

This is one of the pitfalls of modern life unfortunately and is something that we need to be ever vigilant about. Occasionally the problem is more serious (kyphosis – rounded back). If you are concerned then seek professional help.

Achieving good posture when riding will help you to improve your posture in general. Poor posture is related to weak muscles in your 'core' area (the area that includes your pelvis, lower back and belly).

Your horse will find it harder to carry you because basically you are 'on the forehand' (a term that is used to describe a horse's way of going when they are heavy in the front half of their body).

## Solutions

- Ask your assistant to watch you as you stand, walk, sit (unmounted) *and* ride and report what they see.
- Having them take photos and/or videos (before and after shots) will be useful too.
- A good mounted exercise is to experiment with alternating between pushing your chest right out by arching your back to the extreme (picture above) and then slowly changing this position to the opposite of rounding your back in the other direction (picture below).

- Do this a few times and notice at what point you can breathe the easiest.
- Ask your assistant to tell you when your torso is correct, this should correspond with your 'easiest to breathe' position.
- Once you have it remember the feeling.
- Another good exercise is to slowly circle your shoulders backwards. Notice where they are when you stop circling. They should be relaxed and back but you should not have to force them to stay back.

- Next practice riding with your sternum lifted upwards while breathing deeply.
- It is *not* helpful to think about sticking your chest out (because this hollows and stiffens your back). Instead think about taking your shoulders as far away from each other as possible.

- Consider wearing a back support for a while, especially with the stiffer padded section at the front. This will help to keep you upright and at the same time will make you more aware of what your torso is doing (picture below).

- Make sure you look forward between your horse's ears (rather than down at your horse's neck). Look at where you are going.
- Practice exercises that develop your balance and core muscles.

**Balance exercises such as this are covered in the second book in this series, _Horse Rider's Mechanic Workbook 2: Your Balance_.**

- Always check that your saddle is helping you rather than hindering you (see the Horse Rider's Mechanic website article **_Your saddle_**).
- Consider improving your everyday working environment if necessary so that your chair helps you to achieve good posture (i.e. if you work in an office etc.). If possible, reduce the amount of time that you sit in one position while at work.

### 9.3.4: ...torso is tipping forward

This is generally due to the following reasons:

- Nervousness (of the rider).
- The saddle.
- The horse's conformation.

When a rider is nervous they tend to sit in the 'ejector seat' position (picture below) (see **4.3.5: .lower legs are tilting too far back**). Likewise, see the same section if you think it is your saddle that is making you tip forward (or go straight to the Horse Rider's Mechanic website article **Your saddle**).

Tipping forward results in making a rider feel even more insecure. It creates a vicious circle whereby their horse feels the gripping of the thighs and lower legs. So when a rider adopts this position it sends the wrong message to their horse.

*Tipping forward in the upper body is linked to what your lower legs are doing. When your lower legs behave properly you will find it easier to sit up.*

# Solutions

- If this is your problem work on exercises to develop your balance until you feel more secure (see the second book in this series *Horse Rider's Mechanic Workbook 2: Your Balance*).

- You should find that your upper body naturally comes into the upright position once you have improved your position and balance (picture right) and in particular your lower legs.

- If not it may be that the habit is so ingrained that you feel as if you are upright when in fact you are not. In this case you will need the help of your assistant (a friend or instructor) to tell you when you are vertical.

- As with all changes it will feel strange at first to break the habit of leaning forward but as your brain learns the new feeling it starts to feel natural and normal.

- Think about sitting up tall and breathing deeper, visualise the air going down into the very bottom of your lungs.

- Check that your saddle is not tipping you forward. A saddle should be only 1cm (½ inch) higher at the cantle than the pommel when a horse is standing on the flat. Anymore and it will tip you forward (see the Horse Rider's Mechanic website article *Your saddle*).

- The conformation of your horse can add to this problem as some horses are built more 'downhill' than others (see the Horse Rider's Mechanic website article *Your horse*).

# 9.3.5: ...torso is leaning back

This is usually seen in riders who are at the other end of the spectrum to those that lean forward; they are so relaxed they allow themselves to lean back and their legs to come forward.

Riding like this makes it very difficult for a horse to carry you. A horse's back becomes weaker the nearer it gets to the loins (the area directly behind the saddle).

So when a rider puts their weight to the back of the saddle (which is usually what is happening if the legs are forward) *and* leans back (which puts their weight towards the back of the saddle anyway) their horse has to work harder to carry them (picture below).

Also the further back a rider's weight is, the further they are from their horse's centre of gravity and the more difficult it is to ride well, see the Horse Rider's Mechanic website article *Your centre of gravity*.

# Solutions

- The remedy is to sit up and allow your legs to simply hang down from the hip.
- If you are tight through the soft tissues at the front of your hips your need to work on keeping your legs down and back (see **8.3.2: ...lower body is unable to maintain position**).
- Check your saddle to make sure it is not preventing you from sitting upright. In particular make sure that the cantle is not lower than the pommel (remember: your saddle should be 1cm (½ inch) higher at the cantle than the pommel when your horse is standing on the flat).
- Horses that are 'sway backed' (the same condition as lordosis in humans) or 'dippy backed' will also cause the rider to fall into a 'hole' in the middle of their back making it difficult to sit upright.
- In any case professional help should be sought from a saddler. The sway backed horse in this picture (below) has had such help.
- Correct riding can of course help such problems up to a point (because it develops the muscles and makes the back stronger) although if a horse is 'dippy backed' due to age then it will be difficult to improve). If improvement is not occurring then riding that particular horse can become a welfare issue.

# 9.3.6: ...too arched in the lower back

Lordosis of the lower back is a term used to describe a back that has *too much* forward curve although there is no absolute correct amount. It is the same condition as a horse that has a 'sway back'.

All 'normal' lower backs have some forward arch to them but sometimes the lower back arches forward *too* much. A lower back that has a pronounced forward curve *and* is flexible is not really a great detriment to a rider. Flexibility of the lower back is required in order to ride a horse. Without it riding would be very painful indeed.

A lower back that is able to flex backwards and forwards is able to absorb the movement that is happening underneath them.

## *Solutions*

- Too much forward curve will tend to pop the stomach out (picture above). Stronger core muscles help to maintain strength and stability of the lower back so once again riding well is the key to improving this area.
- Riding with a lower back support helps to make you more aware of what your lower back is doing, prevents your stomach from popping out (always a bonus!) and gives support until these muscles become stronger.

# 9.3.7: ...lower back is painful

This is a common problem not least of all because most people do not have the time to ride as much as they would like and therefore develop their core muscles.

You could spend more time at the gym, but riding (well) is one of the best ways of developing your core muscles. So, if you are able to, ride more. A weak torso will often show up as slouching (but not always) and lead to (usually) lower back pain (although you may have lower back pain due to other reasons such as previous injuries, wear and tear etc.).

Upper back pain is common too, especially in people who spend many hours a day sitting in an office environment.

## Solutions

- In my experience lower back pain is *usually* greatly improved by riding but there *are* some situations where riding can make back pain worse. You should get any pain checked out by a professional.
- If a rider with serious back problems insists on riding then the movement and build of their horse becomes of paramount importance.
- I have found that with many riders a lower back support works well to support their core muscles until they develop these muscles and improve their balance (improving the balance also *reduces the amount of effort* required to ride).
- In some riders, particularly if they do not ride frequently enough, a back support can be a great help in the long term too.
- See *9.3.3: ...torso is slouching* for some solutions to upper back pain.

***Working through the ridden balance exercises in Horse Rider's Mechanic Workbook 2: Your Balance will strengthen your core muscles and therefore may help you with back pain.***

# 10: Your head and neck

The human head is very heavy, around 5 kilos or 12 lbs. in most adults and the neck directly affects the positioning of the head.

If you do not position your head correctly then it becomes difficult to carry and your neck and back take the brunt. Correct positioning of the head uses *fewer* muscles to balance the head and therefore less energy. When your head is positioned correctly it is also easier to turn your head (to look around) and it is easier to stretch your neck (lengthen through your spine, which is what you also expect your horse to do!). It is also easier to breath properly.

Keep in mind that some people have a short neck, and some have a long neck and this has a bearing on how their neck 'behaves'. Also the human neck is another one of those areas that has frequently been subjected to wear and tear and/or past injury. So be patient.

## 10.1: Your head should...

*Your head should sit directly above your torso (picture a) and be relatively still but not fixed. You should also be able to comfortably look around when necessary (picture b).*

a  b

## 10.2: However your head may...

- Jut forward.
- Sit back.
- Lean to one side.
- Tip (look) down.
- Wobble.

## 10.3: What you can do if...

### 10.3.1: ...head is incorrectly positioned

Incorrect positioning of the head includes jutting forwards, sitting too far back (i.e. the chin is drawn back too far), tipping (looking) down (picture below) or leaning to one side. All of these positions lead to problems as the rest of your body has to compensate for this heavy weight that is being carried incorrectly.

It will be useful to have your assistant help you with this one, if not try to video yourself riding and work from that.

# *Solutions*

- In halt stretch up through your neck (lengthen your neck) but keep it comfortable, then turn your head slowly from side to side (to look over each shoulder in turn) a few times. Notice if you find it difficult to look either way.
- Then stretch your head forwards and down (chin to chest) and backwards (chin up) a few times.
- Notice how it becomes more difficult to breath when your head is forwards and down.
- Notice how it is also difficult to breathe properly when your head is too far back.
- Lastly stretch your neck laterally by bringing each ear down towards your shoulder in turn a few times.
- Bring your head back to directly above your torso and ask your assistant (if you have one) to tell you when your head is correctly positioned and when it is not. Ask them to take photos or a video of you if you are having particular problems with this area of your body. The pictures should be taken from the side but also from the front or back to check to see if you are putting your head to one side (quite common).
- Notice and remember what it feels like (even though this will not yet feel 'normal').
- Now ride your horse in a circle. Focus on looking around to where you are going (about ¼ to ½ way around the circle) while maintaining this comfortable stretch through your neck.
- Just as with the other areas of your body you may need to really concentrate in order to do this.
- Notice what it feels like to have a longer neck, how much easier it is to see where you are going and how it is now easier to breathe deeply.
- Riders who have their head on one side are often looking down the side of their horse's neck at the side of their horse's face (to try and gauge

their horse). This can come about from a lack of confidence so think about what may be causing this and address these issues if possible (see the Horse Rider's Mechanic website article *Your confidence*).

- The head carried to one side can also be an indication that your torso is not straight. If you are collapsed on the left side of your torso for example your head may tip to one side (picture right).

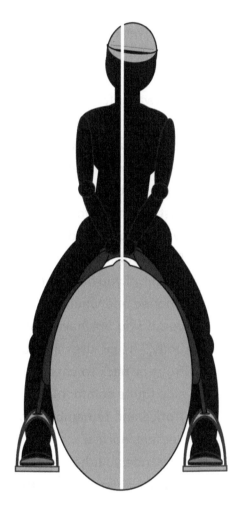

- Concentrate on this area for a while, then do something else, then turn your attention back to this area again and see if you have maintained the 'new improved' head position.
- You should eventually be able to keep your head in the correct position.
- In future it may be a good idea to do some neck movements as a regular part of your warm up routine (before and after you mount).

## 10.3.2: ...head is wobbly

A wobbling head is usually an extension of a torso that moves excessively. Because the movement that is happening underneath you (from your horse) has to go somewhere it will 'pop' out via your head if you cannot absorb it properly into your lower body.

This problem is mainly seen in dressage riders riding big moving horses in sitting trot. It has become so commonplace that some riders do not really see it as a problem, but it should be, because it is a symptom that the rider is not using their body properly.

## *Solutions*

*Correct sitting trot involves stretching downwards with your lower body while simultaneously stretching upwards with your upper body.*

- See **9.3.1: ...torso is moving excessively** and learning to stretch downwards with your lower body while simultaneously stretching upwards with your upper body. Only then can you start to improve your wobbling head. Trying to keep your head still *without* addressing the issue of incorrect absorption through the rest of your body is futile!
- Once you have mastered correct movement absorption (if you still need to improve your head position) see **10.3.1: ...head is incorrectly positioned** and work on the exercises for further improvement.

# 11: Your arms

Humans vary quite a lot in the length of their arms relative to their height. Some people have very short or very long arms. This can make it difficult for some to achieve the ideal position described below.

Everyone should be aware of their own strengths and weaknesses and also any 'quirks' regarding their own body so that they can aim to minimise the effects of any 'problematic body parts' and ride as well as possible.

Shoulder problems are generally very common in people (again usually due to past sporting injuries and/or wear and tear) as are conditions such as 'tennis elbow' and 'carpel tunnel syndrome' (of the wrists) so if you are having such problems it may be difficult for your arm/s to function properly.

Think about getting professional help for any pain related issues if necessary.

## 11.1: Your arms should...

- Have a bend at the elbow and your lower arm should form part of a straight line between your elbow and your horse's mouth (picture a).
- This straight line is important because without it you will not be able to communicate as effectively (via the rein aids) with your horse.
- Hang from your shoulders with your elbows resting just in front of your waist, your shoulders should be relaxed, down and back (picture b) as opposed to tight and 'hunched'.

- Have still (but soft) elbows in sitting trot.
- Have open and closing elbows in rising trot (otherwise your hands will move up and down with your body and will jerk your horse in the mouth).
- Follow the movement of your horse's head in walk and canter.
- Be still and soft. Flapping arms are unsightly and detrimental to your horse. Your horse is attached to the other end of those flapping arms via their mouth!

## 11.2: However your arms may...

- Hang incorrectly.
- Be stiff and unyielding.
- Flap.
- Be too straight.

## 11.3: What you can do if...

### 11.3.1: ...arms are hanging incorrectly

The correct positioning of your arms allows them to be still when necessary and to move when necessary. So, if your elbows rest just in front of your waist, this allows your arms to move forward to 'give' with the reins when necessary. If your elbows are already too far forward you cannot do this. From this position just in front of your waist your arms can also move back slightly to increase the pressure when necessary (picture next page).

Any tension (i.e. anxiety, fear etc.) will tend to draw your shoulders upwards towards your ears. Tension restricts your breathing, stiffens your back and stiffens your arms. This in turn creates tension in your horse.

## Solutions

- Address any issues that may cause tension (see the Horse Rider's Mechanic website article *Your confidence*).
- If this tension is caused by your lifestyle (stress at work etc.) make sure you work to attain a more relaxed state before you mount your horse. Many people ride to 'de-stress'. However you need to make sure you are not transferring your stress to your horse or taking your stress out on your horse!
- Turn your full attention to your shoulders. Lift your shoulders even higher then slowly let them drop, down and back.
- Circling your shoulders backwards can also be very effective if your shoulders are tight and stiff. You could do this each time before and after you mount as part of a warm up routine.
- Notice what it feels like when your shoulders are back and remember the feeling. Notice how much easier it is to breath with your shoulders in this position.
- Do this a few times and then move on to doing something else for a while. Return to thinking about your shoulders and see if you have maintained this new position. Repeat the exercise until it becomes 'second nature'.

## 11.3.2: ...arms are stiff and unyielding

It is *very* important that your arms are still (as opposed to flapping or fidgeting) but *follow* the movement of your horse's head and neck.

Your arms are directly linked to your horse's mouth via your hands, reins and bit (or indeed sensitive nose if your horse is being ridden bitless) so if you do not follow the movement you will be inadvertently pulling/jerking on your horse's mouth (or nose) throughout the cycle of the stride.

This movement (in your horse) occurs because the head and long neck move to help to counterbalance the body.

The movements are different depending on whether your horse is walking, trotting or cantering. A horse's neck/head moves the most in walk, does not move in trot and moves a little in canter so you need to be able to adapt to these changes throughout the various gaits.

Even though a horse's neck/head does not move in trot, when you are rising to the trot, your elbows need to open and close otherwise your hands will lift and drop along with your body. This all takes skill and problems will arise if you try to keep your arms *too* still.

## *Solutions*

- Ask your assistant (if you have one) to make sure you have a straight line from your elbow to your horse's mouth. Ask them to position your arms so that this straight line is achieved, notice what this feels like.
- To learn how to follow the movement of your horse's head in walk, concentrate on the feeling in your arms. Let your horse move your arms rather than vice versa. Aim to have the softest feel possible in your hands.
- You should feel a constant very soft contact with your horse's mouth rather than an increase in pressure followed by a decrease in

pressure (therefore you should *not* feel slack then firm, slack then firm).

- It is important that you perfect this before you move on to faster paces, especially canter, because the head and neck movement of your horse in canter is similar, but it is much easier for you to lose balance and therefore inadvertently pull/jerk your horse in the mouth.

- In *rising* trot your hips are rising up and forwards which means that your shoulders will lift up along with your upper body. So your elbows must open and close softly so that your hands stay in the correct position (pictures a and b previous page).

- A good way to learn how to do this is to use a loose neck strap (loose enough so that you can hold it *and* keep your hands in the correct position) and hold it along with your reins (picture below).

- You will then be able to feel when your hands try to lift along with

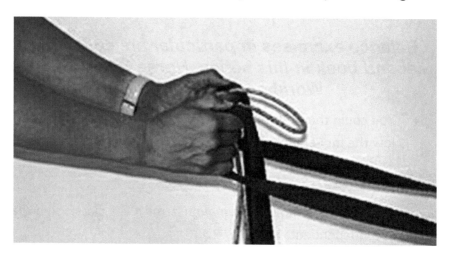

your body as you rise and you will learn what it feels like to instead open and close your elbows as you rise and sit.

- Concentrate on softening your elbows and keeping your hands still as you rise. Once you think you can maintain this position let go of the neck strap and see what happens.

- Notice if you are still keeping your hands still after you have worked on something else for a while and then return to thinking about your hands.
- When you are *sitting* to the trot your arms and hands should stay still but soft.
- In canter you can also use the neck strap to improve your arms because the movement at the base of your horse's neck, which will move the neck strap, will 'show' your hands how to move.
- At the same time you need to concentrate on the feeling in your arms, as you did in walk, until you can follow the movement without pulling on your horse's mouth.
- You will not be able to follow the movement correctly if you still have any issues with your position and balance.
- In this case aim to improve your position (by keeping working through this book until you get it right) and aim to improve your balance.

**Balance exercises in particular are covered in the second book in this series, Horse Rider's Mechanic Workbook 2: Your Balance.**

- You could then return to working on improving how your arms follow the movement of your horse's head and neck in canter.

## 11.3.3: ...arms are flapping

If you have excessive movement in your arms it is a classic sign that your seat is *not* independent.

Flapping arms are a result of your brain trying to counterbalance a loss of balance. If you have worked through this book to this point then you should find that any excessive movement has already been reduced or eradicated. But it may be an 'ingrained habit' so you may need to now turn your attention to this problem in order to eliminate it.

# Solutions

- First of all you need to address any issues with your seat if necessary. Keep working through this book and aim to work through the balance exercises in *Horse Rider's Mechanic Workbook 2: Your Balance.* You should then have attained an independent seat.

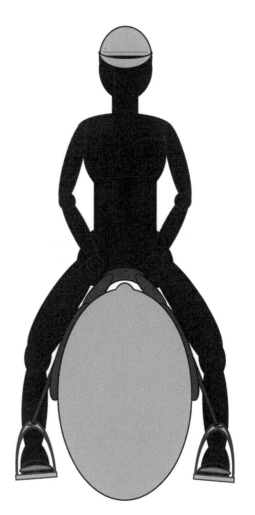

*If your arms flap, the chances are your legs flap too. This is because you do not yet have an independent seat. Trying to force your arms to be still will not work because first of all you need to address the root of the problem - your seat.*

- Think about the feeling of your elbows resting just in front of your waist.
- Notice when they move away from this position and think about why they are doing this.
- Remember: if you are bouncing and your arms start to flap the problem is your seat in general, not your arms in particular. Your flapping arms are simply a symptom of your lack of security and balance.
- In this case go back to working on your seat.

# 12: Your hands

At all times a rider should bear in mind that their horse's mouth (or sensitive nose if the horse is being ridden bitless) is attached to their hands via the reins.

Horses are regularly labelled as having 'a hard mouth' or for 'evading the bit' ('head tossing', 'star gazing', 'behind the bit', 'above the bit', 'opening the mouth', 'crossing the jaw' etc.). In fact there are a *multitude* of descriptions and terms for what horses do to 'avoid a contact' but in fact most if not all of these 'evasions' are caused by a complete lack of empathy from the rider and are due to a rider not having 'good hands'.

Many riders also use their arms and hands to balance themselves because they do not have an independent seat. This is very common and yet quite tragic for a horse. It is no wonder that so many horses try to 'evade the bit' or develop 'learned helplessness' (the scientific term for 'giving up') in the form of becoming 'hard mouthed'.

The term 'good hands' or 'bad hands' is often used to describe a rider. We all like to think that we either have, or are aiming to have, the former. If you have worked hard to gain an independent seat you should be well on the way to developing 'good hands' or at least have achieved the prerequisites. You may be thinking, 'if hands are so important surely the subject should have been covered at the beginning of this book rather towards the end'? But until a rider has an independent seat (i.e. the limbs are able to be moved independently of each other *and* the body, see the Horse Rider's Mechanic website article **An Independent Seat**) the hands cannot be still when required, or move fluidly to give the aids, without the rider experiencing *some* loss of balance.

Until the seat is truly independent, the limbs are used to counterbalance movement in any other part of the body (hence the earlier example of when a 'beginner rider' uses their legs, their hands tend to shoot up in the air). In more experienced riders these moments of loss of balance are much more subtle but they may still be there.

Having correctly positioned 'still' (but soft) hands is just the start. Developing more and more 'feel' (see the Horse Rider's Mechanic website article **Feel and timing?**) is something that takes time to achieve. In the same way that a masseur might take years to develop 'feel' in their hands, a rider also needs time and experience to develop 'feel'. Once the hands are still a rider begins to become much more aware of what is happening in general and can control the pressure that they exert on the reins. This is then the start of developing 'feel'.

In the future gadgets that measure the pressure that a rider's hands and arms exert on the reins will be readily available. They will go a long way to improving riders for the benefit of their horse.

Hands vary a lot from person to person. Think about how some people can draw, sew etc. easily whereas some people cannot. This is to do with the level of 'fine motor skills' that a person has. Everyone can improve their fine motor skills but there is a limit and it is much easier for some than others. Also the length of your arms and the head position of your horse will affect the position of your hands slightly.

## 12.1: Your hands should...

- Be positioned with the backs facing outwards.
- Be in line with your forearms (and in line with the reins).
- Have the thumbs resting on top of the reins and the thumbs should be uppermost.

- Be about 10 cm (4 inches) apart, just above the withers and in front of the pommel of the saddle.
- Stay on the corresponding side of your horse's neck i.e. (rather than cross the mid line of your horse's neck).
- Be soft and still (have 'feel') but be effective.
- Slow the horse down *and* move the horse's shoulders sideways.

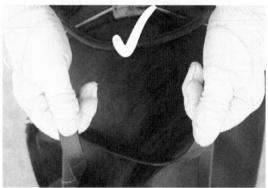

## 12.2: However your hands may...

- Be unable to maintain position.
- Move incorrectly.
- Be hard and heavy.

## 12.3: What you can do if...

### 12.3.1: ...hands are unable to maintain position

#### *Solutions*

- An excellent exercise to improve your hands is to place a gadget such as a whip, straight stick or piece of dowel under your thumbs as you ride (picture next page).
- This exercise 'retrains' hands that are incorrectly positioned.

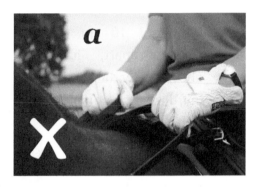

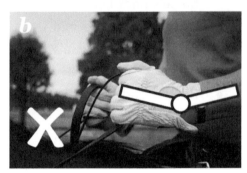

Common problems with hands include turning the hands downward, as if riding a bike, (picture a). This turns the elbows out and rotates the shoulder blades off of the back. Other common problems include 'cocking' the wrists upwards (picture b) and having one hand sitting higher than the other.

- When rising to the trot with a stick under your thumbs in this way you will notice if your hands lift with you (incorrect) and you may find that your shoulders try to twist (the twist actually originates in your torso) to 'help' you get up and out of the saddle.

- Once your hands can be kept still (which takes a fair bit of core body strength) the stick will stay still and level. You may notice that your core muscles have to work a bit harder at first. For this reason I also use this exercise to straighten people if they have crookedness in other areas of their body (see *7.3.2: ...hips are crooked*).
- By carrying out this exercise you will learn a new (correct) feeling and when the stick is taken away, your hands should remain still, at least for a while, in which case keep repeating the exercise until your hands can stay still without effort.

## 12.3.2: ...hands are moving incorrectly

Your hands should be still and you should have full control of them in order for you to convey clear messages to your horse via the rein aids.

If your arms move then your hands will too. These problems are linked and the solutions are also linked. If you have worked through *11: Your arms* you should be well on the way to improving your hands.

I often come across riders that 'fiddle' with their reins. In many cases this is due to them not understanding how to hold their reins properly and/or how to shorten and lengthen them properly. Because this leads to a feeling of insecurity (due to them not feeling 'in control' of their hands, reins or horse) they tend to 'grapple' with their reins.

### Solutions

- Riding with a neck strap, as described in *11.3.2: ...arms are stiff and unyielding,* will help you to 'retrain' your hands to be more still. Use it for sitting trot and rising trot until you can stop your hands from moving inadvertently.
- Riding with a stick under your thumbs as described in *12.3.1: Hands unable to maintain position* will also help.
- Learning how to hold the reins properly and how to shorten and lengthen them quickly with ease, is an *essential* skill for a rider.

- When you hold the reins they should sit above your little fingers, between the second and third knuckles. They should come out of your hands above your index fingers (again between the second and third knuckles) and your thumbs should rest on top of them. The 'excess' part of the reins (that comes out of the top of your

hands) should fall *forwards* and down the *inside* of one of the reins (between the horse's neck and the rein (picture above).
- The backs of your hands should face outwards and your hands should be relaxed unless you are giving an aid.
- Shortening you reins should be done in such a way that you do not change the pressure on the reins. Therefore it is incorrect (and un-safe) to shorten the reins by simply 'walking' your fingers down the reins.

The safest and correct way to shorten the reins is to grasp the top of the left rein with the thumb and forefinger of the right hand (above the left hand not below) (picture a).

Then slide the right hand down the rein (picture b).

Then release the left rein from between the thumb and forefinger (picture c).

Repeat for the other rein.

A well practiced rider can do this very quickly and without changing the consistency of the feeling between the reins and their horse's mouth.

### 12.3.3: ...hands are hard and heavy

Your hands should have a very light but steady contact with your horse's mouth and your fingers should curl gently around the reins. You need to take care that your fingers are neither fully open (picture right) or tightly clenched. There should not be tension in your wrists.

If your hands are too 'closed' you will not be able to make subtle movements with your fingers when giving the aids. Your horse will also feel the tension in your hands. If your fingers are too open, again you will not be able to make subtle movements with your fingers and you will drop the reins too easily (i.e. if your horse makes a sudden movement with their head).

People who ride with hard heavy hands often do so because that is how they were taught to ride. Certain methods of riding teach that a rider should be able to feel a 'strong contact' on each rein as they ride. Imagine what this must feel like to a horse's sensitive mouth!

Typically horses that have been ridden in this way are called 'hard mouthed'. This is a term that unfortunately blames the horse rather than the rider. A horse has no choice but to learn to ignore the rein pressure if there is no way of gaining relief from it. Usually once a rider is reeducated and understands that it is incorrect (and unethical) to ride with a 'strong contact' then learning to soften the rein contact becomes quite easy. So the initial change has to take place in the riders brain! After that it is just a matter of learning a new feel.

# Solutions

- If you like mental imagery you might like to imagine that you are holding a very small animal in each hand. Clenching too tight will squash the animal and opening your hand will drop it.
- Notice how much tension you have in your hands, wrists and forearms. If you are riding with tension in these areas you will be conveying this tension to your horse.

- On a slack rein (so that you do not upset your horse and if it is safe to do so) increase the tension in your forearms and hands and then relax it, as you did in other areas of your body) (pictures right).

- When you think you have reduced the tension in this area work on something else for a while and then return to thinking about your hands, wrists and forearms again to see if you have kept them relaxed or if you have tightened them again.
- Keep repeating this exercise until you can maintain a more relaxed state without having to think about it.
- You will need to perfect this so that you can eventually improve the application of the rein aids.

**The correct application of the aids is covered in the third book in this series, Horse Rider's Mechanic Workbook 3: The Aids.**

# 13: Your upper body

This section looks at your upper body *as a whole*. It is a recap of the previous sections and has some further information.

## 13.1: Your upper body should...

- *Follow* the movement of your horse's back *and* absorb any movement that does not travel downwards into your pelvis/lower back.
- Stretch upwards as your lower body stretches downwards (the upper body should be in line with the classic ear, shoulder, hip, ankle alignment).
- Be responsible for giving the 'slow down' aids and for positioning the 'front half' of your horse. Your hands *decrease* your horse's speed when applied together and move your horse's forequarters sideways when required; this is covered in detail in **Horse Rider's Mechanic Workbook 3: The Aids**.

## 13.2: However your upper body may...

- Be unable to follow and absorb the movement.
- Be unable to maintain position.
- Be unable to give the aids effectively.

## 13.3: What you can do if...

### 13.3.1: ...upper body is unable to follow and absorb the movement

Your upper body has to work as a cohesive unit, that includes your torso, arms, hands and head, to follow and absorb the movement of your horse.

If you are riding correctly most of the movement of your horse is absorbed into your lower body but your upper body will also absorb some of the movement.

This following and absorbing action of the upper body takes place mainly in your lower back area, while your upper back and head stay relatively still. At the same time your arms move in time with the movements of your horse's head and neck in walk and canter. In trot your hands stay still.

This is very complex and can only be achieved if the lower body is working correctly to absorb *as much of the movement as possible.*

## Solutions

- If you are unable to follow and absorb the movement while keeping your upper body tall and relatively still, check your lower body once more. Then concentrate on letting your horse move you rather than vice versa, while drawing yourself up through your upper body (picture right).

- This is a complex process but easily understood once it is explained properly. Once you have it learned this skill you should never forget it.

***The next book in this series, Horse Rider's Mechanic Workbook 2: Your Balance, explains in detail how you should move your seat so that you follow the movement of your horse's back.***

## 13.3.2: ...upper body is unable to maintain position

A rider needs to stretch up through their upper body at the same time as stretching down through their lower body, this is no easy feat because it has to be accomplished at the same time as balancing on a complex moving animal. The lower body *has* to be correct first (picture left), before the upper body can be correct. This very important fact is often forgotten (or never discovered) by a rider, to their detriment.

### Solutions

- If you cannot 'sit tall' through your upper body without bouncing (in trot or canter) then the problem is likely to be in your lower body.
- In this case, forget (for now) trying to sit tall and concentrate once more on your lower body, correct any faults, then return to lifting through your sternum.
- If you feel yourself starting to 'lose it' again go back to engaging your lower legs and make sure that you are 'anchored' on your horse once more.

# 13.4: Your upper body – a recap

Your upper body is responsible for giving the 'slow down' aids *and* for positioning the 'front half' of your horse i.e. for moving the forequarters - shoulders, head and neck - sideways ('lateral movements'). This is all covered in detail in *Horse Rider's Mechanic Workbook 3: The Aids.* At this stage your aim should be to position yourself as well as possible so that you can work through the balance exercises in *Horse Rider's Mechanic Workbook 2: Your Balance.*

Then your flexibility (if you were stiff), your riding fitness (if you were unfit) and your stability (if you had poor balance) will all have improved.

This will lead to clearer more concise aids. So, improving your upper body involves:

- Identifying any problems.
- Making sure that your *lower body* is correctly positioned and is absorbing movement as much as possible and has 'engaged' lower legs.
- Making sure that your torso is as still, straight and upright as possible (but not stiff).
- Making sure that that you are able to absorb the movement of your horse through your lower back.
- Making sure that your head is set straight and does not wobble.
- Making sure that your arms and hands are able to follow the movements of your horse's head when necessary.
- Making sure that your hands are relatively still and are sensitive to your horse's mouth.
- Making sure that your hands give clear concise aids to your horse.

# 14: Your whole body

Finally we bring *all* of the parts of your body together to work as a whole. Hopefully, in terms of *position* you will now be feeling much better. But be patient, a correct position is only *part* of what is needed in order to ride well. A good position sets your body up so that it can perform as well as possible. Not everyone can achieve a perfect position due to idiosyncrasies in their body (we all have them to a lesser or greater extent) but we can all *aim* to position our body as well as possible.

## 14.1: Your whole body should...

Viewed from the side a straight line should pass from your ear through your shoulder, hip and ankle. Another straight line should pass from your elbows, through your hands, to your horse's mouth. Viewed from the front or back your torso should be directly above your horse, a straight line should pass from your chin, through your breast bone, belly button and pubic bone which should align with the centre of your horse's back. Your legs should hang equally down each side of your horse with your stirrups being of equal length (picture next page).

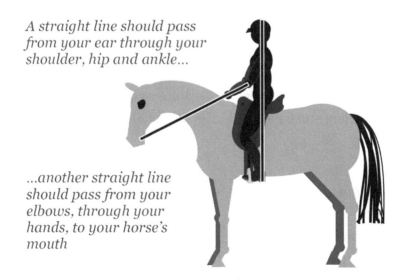

*A straight line should pass from your ear through your shoulder, hip and ankle...*

*...another straight line should pass from your elbows, through your hands, to your horse's mouth*

Your whole body should also allow you to fulfil *your* potential as a rider (whether that is just enjoying your horse as a companion or competing, or both). At the same time you should aim to be the best 'passenger' possible for your horse (in the sense of enabling your horse to be able to carry you better).

Lastly you should have an independent seat. The various areas of your body should be able to work independently but harmoniously, giving the illusion of effortlessness.

# 14.2: However your whole body may...

- Be unable to follow and absorb the movement.
- Be unable to maintain position.
- Be unable to give the aids effectively.

# 14.3: What you can do if...

## 14.3.1: ...whole body is unable to follow and absorb the movement

It can be frustrating when you really want to ride well but your body is difficult to coordinate. Riding involves carrying out various actions simultaneously. The coordination required is quite significant and that requires correct positioning and balance to be in place beforehand.

### Solutions

- An independent seat takes time to develop. Correct positioning is only the start.
- Next your need to improve your balance. Then your coordination will improve.

***The next book in this series, Horse Rider's Mechanic
Workbook 2: Your Balance, will improve your balance
which will in turn improve your seat.***

## 14.3.2: ...whole body is unable to maintain position

Becoming an effective rider takes time to develop because riding requires various coordination based skills. These skills have to be learned and built on, one by one.

   People that are more experienced but have been riding incorrectly positioned will eventually break bad habits once they are shown a new way of positioning their body, especially if the reason for changing the position makes sense to them. The fact that they already have some of the coordination based skills that are required to ride well means that they can usually progress quickly.

## *Solutions*

- Review and check your position every time you first get on your horse. Throughout your ride realign yourself whenever you get the chance (for example when you and your horse are having a 'breather').
- If you are having problems with your riding always start by reviewing your position (and then your balance).
- Keep in mind that you should not expect your horse to be straight and balanced if you cannot be straight and balanced yourself.
- Periodically run through your cards while mounted so that you can check the various parts of your body.
- Make sure you do this now (before moving on to ***Horse Rider's Mechanic Workbook 2: Your Balance***) because adjustments to your upper body may have inadvertently caused your lower body to revert to bad habits.

# 14.4: Your whole body – a recap

Everyone has a certain amount of potential. That amount of potential varies enormously from person to person.

Striving to ride as well as possible (for you and your body and all of its individual 'peculiarities') is the best approach rather than judging your personal progress against other people who may or may not have 'problem' body parts. Everyone has their own set of idiosyncrasies. It is whether you manage to ride as well as possible *despite* your body's peculiarities that matters. Don't 'beat yourself up' if you are trying your best!

Practice makes perfect' is a common saying. I would say 'practice brings you nearer to perfection' because I believe that perfection is not attainable but you should aim to be the best you can be.

By riding as much as possible, by taking any sensible opportunity to ride different horses (and in particular different *types* of horses) and by always striving to learn more you *will* continue to improve.

This improvement in skills will be appreciated by your horse, who in turn will improve his or her way of going as you become easier to carry (due to your better position and balance) and as you learn to give clearer aids. So improving your whole body involves:

- Identifying any problems.
- Making sure that your *lower body* and your *upper body* are correctly positioned and are absorbing the movement created by your horse.
- Making sure that the two halves of your body are cooperating by carrying out their respective functions while working together for the benefit of your seat, your riding *and* your horse.

Now that you have worked your way through this book you should be feeling much better in terms of your position.

The information so far has been about where you should place the various parts of your body when riding and what you should aim to feel.

*Horse Rider's Mechanic Workbook 2: Your Balance is about how you can improve your balance so that you maximise the potential of having correct positioning and good balance. This will greatly improve your seat. You can start reading this book (for free) on www.horseridersmechanic.com*

*Remember: if there is anything you do not understand or need help with after reading this book (or the others in this series) post a question on the Horse Rider's Mechanic Facebook page: www.facebook.com/horseridersmechanic*

# Final thoughts

We hope you have enjoyed this book and that you have gained some insightful information about your position.

Remember, it is a good idea to go back through this book from time to time because bad habits have a way of influencing you without you even realising!

*You can contact us via the Facebook page:*
*www.facebook.com/horseridersmechanic*

*.... by posting a question. That way others benefit as well. If you would rather remain anonymous (to the other readers) you can PM me as long as you are happy for me to share the problem on the page (with your identity removed).*

*Don't forget to keep up with the new articles on www.horseridersmechnic.com where you can join the mailing list and be kept up to date. You can also start reading (for free) the next book in this series Horse Rider's Mechanic Workbook 2: Your Balance on www.horseridersmechanic.com.*

# Our other publications

## A horse is a horse of course: A guide to equine behaviour

This publication will teach you about horse behaviour, in particular those aspects of horse behaviour that relate to their management and training. It also includes information about how horses learn and it explains many of the scientific concepts and terminology used to describe horse behaviour and horse training.

This publication will give you a thorough introduction to this subject, starting with how horses behave when in

a natural setting. Using the knowledge gained from reading this book you can then aim to provide an environment that is as close to natural as possible when keeping horses in captivity.

The information in this book is scientifically based but is written so that it is understandable and applicable whatever your background. Everyone from complete novices to very experienced horse people will gain invaluable information from this publication.

## Horse pasture management

Your pasture is a valuable resource, to you, your horses and to the wider environment. Pasture, if managed well, provides an enriching environment for your horses. However if poor management systems are used, too much grazing pressure can lead to a downward spiral of land degradation resulting in pasture loss, soil erosion and weed infestation etc.

This publication explains the benefits of good pasture management and then shows you how to manage your land in a way that is a win-win situation for all concerned.

It will also show you how to integrate good pasture management strategies, along with your property infrastructure, into an efficient time and energy saving system called *The Equicentral System*.

## Understanding horses and pasture

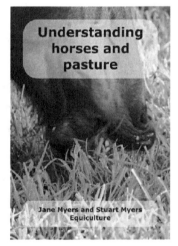

Millions of years of evolution have created a symbiotic relationship between equines (and other grazing animals) and grasslands. Our aim as horse owners and as custodians of the land should be to replicate that relationship on our property as closely as possible.

By managing our land effectively we can ensure that the environment and our horses achieve optimum health. To manage our pasture well, we first need to understand it and the relationship that equines and other grazing animals have with it.

There is a belief that pasture is not good or is even dangerous for certain types of horses. However with the correct knowledge all these issues can be addressed and managed to the benefit of both horses and pasture.

Horse owners can improve the condition of their land and play an important part in increasing biodiversity. To do this horse owners need to be aware of horse grazing behaviour and gain a basic understanding of pasture plants so that they can manage their pastures and the grazing of them. All horses benefit from grazing; it is what they have evolved to do for a large part of their day. In turn, grass and other pasture plant species have evolved to benefit from periods of grazing and periods of rest. Managing horses and pasture effectively is to the benefit of both.

## Horse property planning

All too often a horse property is developed without a proper plan. This usually results in extra work and wasted money. This publication will provide you with the information and framework you need to plan your horse property well. It deals with planning a property from scratch or making changes to a property that already has some facilities in place. It covers the seven factors you should consider before even starting your plan. It then covers the subject of infrastructure such as where fences, stables, yards, arenas, laneways and driveways should be situated.

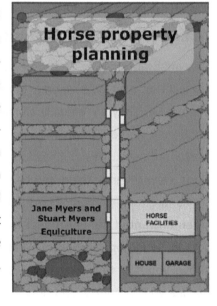

Finally this publication explains how to bring everything together into an efficient time and energy saving system (*The Equicentral System*) which has tremendous benefits for yourself, your horses and the environment.

## Buying a horse property

Buying a horse property is probably the most expensive and important purchase you will ever make. So it is very important that you get it right. There are many factors to consider and there may be compromises that have to be made. This guide to buying a horse property will help you to make many of those very important decisions.

Decisions include such as whether to buy developed or undeveloped land? Whether to buy a smaller property nearer the city or a larger property in a rural area.

This publication will help you with what to look out for and what to avoid when selecting a property and provides you with a list of questions that you should ask yourself about potential properties.

## Manure, water and vegetation on a horse property

This publication covers the three seemingly diverse subjects on a horse property, manure, water and vegetation. They are actually all linked and require good management in order to be an asset to your horse property. This publication is in three sections, each covering the different subjects.

Manure management shows you how to turn an often unwanted waste product into a valuable asset on your horse property. Water management shows you how to manage the water entering and leaving your property, and how to ensure that it is clean and healthy. Vegetation management shows you how to manage the trees, bushes and plants on your property for benefits that go beyond yourself and your animals. Good management of all three areas will enhance the environment for yourself, your horses and wildlife.

## Riding arenas and training yards

This publication will help you to make important decisions about any riding/training surfaces you plan to construct. Some factors to consider include:

- How often will you use this surface?
- Are you planning to have an arena or a training yard, or both?
- Will you carry out the work yourself (DIY) or use a professional company?
- Is it to be outdoor or indoor, or partially covered?
- Will this area be used solely for riding and training or can it also be used for other purposes?

This publication will help you to ask the right questions of any potential contractors and will help you to give contractors the right directions about what you really want. If you plan to DIY your arena or training yard this publication will help you to decide if that is the best way to proceed and if you do, what the most important considerations are.

## Stables, yards and shelters

With regard to facilities on a horse property, stables, holding yards and shelters are perhaps second only to fences when it comes to importance for most horse owners. This publication will help you to decide just what is needed in your particular circumstances. It will also help you to decide what type of materials to use for these facilities and where they should be situated on your horse property.

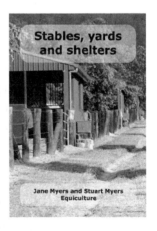

The publication will also show you how you can integrate your holding yards into an efficient money, time and energy saving management system (*The Equicentral System*).

## Horse property fences and gates

Secure and safe fences and gates are a 'must have' on any horse property. They are also one of the biggest expenses when setting up a horse property so it is very important that you get it right the first time round because any mistakes will be very costly.

This publication covers all aspects of this important subject including fence materials, specifications, safety considerations and the layout of fences and gates on a horse property. The pros and cons off different fence types are discussed and gateways (a potentially dangerous area) and their positioning are described in detail.

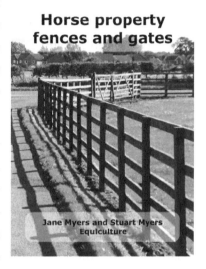

## Horse properties - a management guide

This 49 page book is a short overview of our one day workshop on this subject. It covers many sustainable horsekeeping issues and is full colour with numerous photos and diagrams..

**These books are available as ebooks and printed from the shops on our websites, www.horseridersmechanic.com and www.equiculture.com.au**

**New books are becoming available all the time, make sure you sign up for our mailing list while you are on our websites so that you find out when they are published.**

CPSIA information can be obtained at www.ICGtesting.com
Printed in the USA
LVOW01s1944190615

443144LV00007B/21/P